BUFFET
— A N D —
PARTY
FOOD

BUFFET
AND
PARTY FOOD

ELIZABETH COX

Contents

INTRODUCTION 6

PASTRIES 24

PÂTÉS & TERRINES 37

BREAD 44

VEGETABLES 57

FISH 62

MEAT 68

DIPS & EXTRAS 80

DESSERTS 86

INDEX 94

First published in 1986 by
Octopus Books Limited as
Finger and Fork Food.

This edition published in 1989 by
The Hamlyn Publishing Group Limited,
a division of the Octopus Publishing Group,
Michelin House, 81 Fulham Road, London SW3 6RB

ISBN 0 600 56471 1

Produced by Mandarin Offset.
Printed and bound in Hong Kong.

We Request the Pleasure

Whether you are catering for a grand buffet party or for a more informal get-together, the recipes in this book will help you to be an expert hostess. Some of them are ideal for pre-dinner drinks, while others, if used in well-balanced

combinations (see pages 22-23), are designed to be as substantial as a set meal. There are also many valuable hints on advance preparation and the presentation of food.

To ensure that your party will be a success, first define the type of party you want to give, then plan each stage carefully, and get ahead as much as you can with the preparation.

Lists are the key to good planning. Give yourself plenty of time at this stage and prepare a careful breakdown of what you need to borrow or hire, which dishes you can prepare in advance, and of course, a calculation of quantities of food and drink required. You might also draw a plan of the rooms in which the guests are going to circulate, checking that you will be having the areas of arrival, eating and drinking, in a layout which does not cause congestion.

When sending invitations, add a personal touch by writing in the guests' names and adding an attractive border in a coloured pen. Indicate clearly on the invitation whether it is extended to include a partner – an unexpected arrival of enthusiastic partygoers on the doorstep can ruffle the most proficient of hostesses. Most invitations can be sent out four weeks before the date.

The cost of giving a party may seem daunting, but you can stretch a budget by avoiding expensive foods. Look to see which ingredients are in season, if any stores are promoting particular ranges, and most of all, be slightly adaptable when you are actually out shopping. The visual impact of a buffet is paramount to its enjoyment, and you should be thinking about garnishes and decorations at these initial stages. Plan to have a variety of shapes, textures, colours and flavours. In particular avoid too many pastry-based recipes or those with rich, creamy mixtures. Moderate highly-seasoned foods, so that they do not devastate your guests' tastebuds! As hostess you deserve to enjoy the party too – so devise a menu based on plenty of advance preparation, and do not try to be over-ambitious. Inevitably there is more to do on the day itself than you had foreseen.

Serve as many of the foods as you can cut into individual portions. If you have turkey on the menu, make sure you carve sufficient slices to serve everyone, or enlist a volunteer to keep an eye on when the slices are running low and to carve some more.

Advance Preparation

The next important step is to work out a rough timetable in order to leave the minimum of work for the day itself.

Choux buns, unbaked flan cases and quantities of rubbed in fat and flour ready for pastry making, all freeze well. Many of the dessert recipes in this book will freeze, either with or without their final decorations. Wherever you can, divide recipes into individual portions before freezing, e.g. cut a firm terrine into slices and freeze with waxed paper in between each layer. Make sure that you label each food clearly so that you can recognize it easily and remember to leave ample time for the foods to thaw before the party.

Slices of lemon, orange or lime can be open frozen on non-stick silicone paper, then packed in freezer bags. Used straight from the freezer, they will save time on the day. For a special touch, put strips of orange or lemon peel, quarters of citrus fruit slices, mint sprigs, cocktail cherries, olives and rose petals into the ice tray before filling with water. If freezer space is in short supply, certain super-markets, off-licences and freezer centres sell packs of ice cubes. At home these will keep solid for several hours in a freezer box filled with newspaper. These frozen cubes cool the drink and garnish it at the same time.

Sandwiches can be cut the night before, wrapped in alumi-nium foil and stored in the refrigerator. If using moist fillings, spread the butter generously to the edges to pre-vent the bread becoming soggy. Brown bread is easier to slice if it is put in the freezer for about 1 hour until firm. Many dips will keep in the refrigerator for several hours and accompanying vegetables can be prepared and stored separately in plastic bags in the refrigerator overnight. Cocktail sausages and bacon rolls can be cooked, drained thoroughly on paper towels, then stored overnight in a sealed container. Thread cocktail sticks with cheese cubes, fruit, olives etc., several hours ahead. Prepare salad dress-ings and keep them chilled in closed jars, chop nuts and herbs and de-seed grapes.

Brief freezing ⎡F⎤ and/or advance preparation details ⎡A⎤ are included where possible.

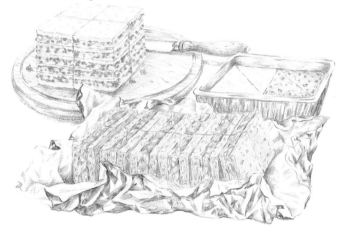

Setting the Scene

However informal your party is, the special attention you put into presenting the buffet table attractively will go a long way towards its overall success. Arrange everything within easy reach. Dishes which require spoons are best at the front of the table, as are shallow plates of food. Any taller pedestal dishes should sit further back on the table. You can make a raised section at the back of the table by putting stout boxes under the tablecloth. An old blanket on the table under the boxes will stop them slipping. At a large gathering, repeat some of the food displays, so that guests can approach from either end of the table. Arrange meats and fish in the centre of the table, and the salads and side dishes towards the outside edges.

Flowers show that you have taken care over setting the scene. Keep arrangements low if they are likely to intrude upon the serving area and avoid any foliage which trails across the tablecloth. There are alternatives to using fresh flowers – silk flowers make an excellent display. The stems of most silk flowers can be gently looped back to temporarily shorten them. An arrangement combining fresh flowers with fake berries and foliage is another possibility. Wide ribbons and large-leafed foliage make effective fillers to save on the number of flowers you need. One important detail – leave strongly-scented fresh flowers out of your arrangement as these can become too intrusive in a party atmosphere. If fresh flowers are especially expensive, a few smallish container plants, such as azalea, pelargonium and cyclamen will brighten the table. Improvise with containers for arrangements; try using baskets, fruit bowls and painted food tubs.

Identification tags are a good idea for foods cooked in pastry and sandwiches, where the fillings are concealed. Cut a triangular flag from a piece of paper and attach with glue to a cocktail stick, with a handwritten description of the food.

To ease crowding, provide separate tables, or a trolley, for starters, desserts, cutlery, plates and coffee. Wrap each guest's cutlery in a napkin to save time on the day.

A Good Spread

Double-check which foods will be served in which dishes to save yourself a last-minute panic. Larger pastry and more fragile desserts which require slicing should go on flat plates; gravy and sauce boats will need a plate under them, and you will need a number of ramekin or glass dishes for individual desserts. Heat foods in a dish you can serve them in wherever possible. To set off a plain china dish, you can place it on top of a larger patterned one. Equally important is the arrangement of foods on the table in relation to each other. Contrasts of texture and colour give visual interest and a brightly coloured dish will liven up a duller one close by.

Look into unusual ways to serve foods: a fruit salad in a melon basket, or cocktail bites stuck into a cooking apple, cabbage, or French loaf.

If you will be providing a cheeseboard, whole or half cheeses are often more economical than several smaller pieces, and they dry out less quickly. Introduce some green grapes, a jug of celery sticks, or some sprigs of fresh herbs, such as rosemary, as a garnish, and the cheeseboard will look doubly appetizing. Offer a variety of cheese biscuits to accompany. If you can, discreetly remove the cheese course once the guests have finished; you will save it from absorbing other flavours and in particular cigarette smoke, as well as from becoming warm and sweaty.

Curls, pats or butter balls should be put in iced water before the party and garnished with sprigs of parsley just before setting out on the table. If you are serving plain cuts of bread, warm them first in the oven at a low temperature for 10 minutes, then arrange the pieces in overlapping slices in a basket for an attractive display. If you are serving rolls, mix a variety of shapes and textures in the same selection. Line the bread dish or basket with a napkin, ruffle the edges and even bread takes on a special party style.

Perfect Portions

One of the easiest ways to guide people on how much to take is to indicate portions by spacing the garnish on the foods at appropriate intervals. Avoid putting a garnish in the centre, though, which is difficult to cut through.

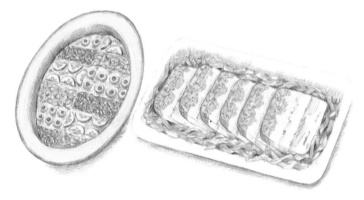

Some foods, however, such as terrines, are best pre-cut into slices before serving. Cut through quiches, pies and whole soft cheeses also, so that portions are not left to chance. Slice a hard cheese such as Cheddar and include individually wrapped cheeses on the cheeseboard.

Cocktail sticks are indispensable for finger and fork food occasions. You can pierce a selection of sandwich quarters on to sticks, to enable a tasty assortment to be picked up in one

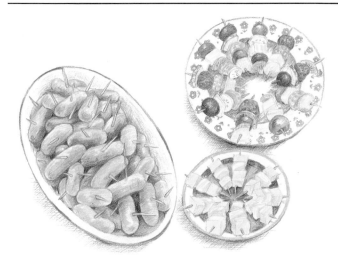

go. For some parties, such as those where guests have bought tickets, it is more convenient to serve a selection of pre-arranged foods on each plate.

Small individual desserts and decorations on large desserts will give your guests an idea of portions.

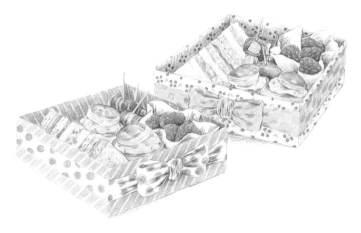

For children-sized portions, use small boxes as containers for sandwiches, vol-au-vents and tit-bits on cocktail sticks. Cover the boxes with pretty paper and tie a ribbon round them.

Salad Accompaniments

A couple of good knives, and possibly a canelle knife, are important assets for the hostess. By cutting salad vegetables in imaginative ways you will create highly presentable results from the simplest of ingredients.

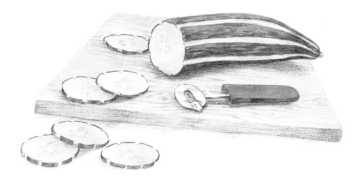

A fine, serrated knife cuts tomatoes into slices with ease. Alternatively, you can turn whole tomatoes into waterlillies – cut a zig-zag through to the middle around the waist of the tomato, using a small sharp knife; separate the two halves and sprinkle chopped herbs, onion or egg in the centre of each. Cut carrots and mushrooms into paper-thin slices; or use a fondant or tiny pastry cutter to stamp out carrot patterns. A canelle knife can be used to cut grooves down the length of a cucumber, which give an attractive edging when the cucumber is sliced.

Salads should include as many different shapes as you can think of. Scrape cucumber skin with a fork, then slice it into

batons instead of the usual slices. Lightly blanch leeks and separate them into rings. Cube beetroot and peppers. Cut chicory, carrots, spring onions and young courgettes on the diagonal – it makes all the difference.

Shred cabbage and combine both red and white. Grate celeriac or cut it into very thin slices. When you include apple slices, you need to brush them first with lemon juice to prevent discoloration. Do the same with avocado slices and use a stainless steel knife for cutting them. A fan of avocado slices makes an attractive centrepiece to a salad. Bring a freshness to your salads at any time of the year by using clever combinations of flavour, texture and colour. In winter, root vegetables will supplement expensive salad produce. This is the season for adding plenty of other ingredients, too – dried fruits, nuts, olives, gherkins, rice and pasta – to stretch the basics.

In summer, arrange overlapping slices of tomato and sprinkle with chopped onion, or add clusters of watercress. Brighten a courgette-based salad with slices of red-skinned apples and walnuts, then add a border of endive. Turn a bean salad into an eye-catching three-colour arrangement by mixing butter beans, red beans and French beans.

Finishing Touches

With finger food, presentation starts from the time you pipe elegant whirls of savoury mixtures on to canapés and ends with your choice of garnish.

Herbs and vegetables are two of the most attractive garnishes of all. Finely snip cress and chives with scissors; chop parsley on a board; and extract a few green leaves from the head of celery. Make 'bouquets' of watercress by trimming the ends of a small bunch fairly short and arranging these 'bouquets' along the sides of a plate. Individual herb leaves, such as dill, coriander and flat-leaved parsley make good garnishes, too.

By piping soft toppings on to savoury bases you immediately enhance your display. Use a star vegetable nozzle for fuller designs or use an 8-point star, or shell cake icing nozzle to add lines, stars and shells. Complete the effect by adding a delicate garnish, such as half a cucumber slice inserted at a 45° angle, a sliver of red, yellow or green pepper or even just a sprinkling of paprika to liven up the colour.

Bread can be used as a display medium. Enclose delicious ingredients in finger sandwiches, as shown in Asparagus rolls (page 49). Alternatively, spread a soft mixture on to slices of bread cut lengthways from an unsliced loaf. Roll up and wrap in cling film or aluminium foil. Put in the refrigerator for several hours (or overnight), then cut across into 2.5 cm (1 inch) pinwheels.

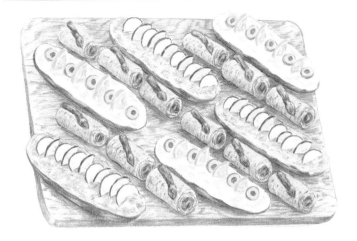

Garnish platters of food with radish roses or waterlillies. To make roses, cut off a narrow slice from the root end of a radish, then cut thin 'petals' from stem to root, alternating the rows as you work. For waterlillies, make 4-8 small deep cuts, crossing over in the centre of the radish at the root end. Leave both roses and waterlillies in iced water for several hours to open out. To make carrot rolls, scrape, and slice carrots into paper-thin lengths with a vegetable peeler. Roll up, fasten with cocktail sticks and leave in iced water. To make gherkin fans, simply make about four lengthways cuts through the gherkin almost through to the pointed end. Gently ease apart. Cut lemon and cucumber butterflies – halve a thin slice, then cut towards the centre from the outer edge, keeping the middle cut joined. Gently open out.

For desserts, glacé cherries and angelica can be cut into shapes to make a flower and stalk, or make a geometrical design from angelica alone. Grate a chilled block of chocolate; or cut a strawberry almost to its root and open it out into a fan. On smooth surfaced desserts you can pipe a design with melted chocolate (thinned with a little water, glycerine or flavourless salad oil, if necessary). Use a greaseproof paper icing bag, snip a fraction off the point and pipe several lines. If you draw the point of a knife through the chocolate before it sets, you will get a feathered design.

Cheers!

As hostess you want to keep the serving of drinks as easy as you can. Two effort-saving ideas are to serve one type of drink throughout the party and to advise guests to help themselves after the first drink.

Depending upon the occasion, you can buy wine in a box, decant sherry as the aperitif, top up a large jugful of Buck's Fizz, or have some warming mulled wine at the ready – with a little thought given to it beforehand the bar will run as smoothly as the buffet. Champagne should not be opened

until just before it is served, so if it is for a toast enlist some assistance. Keep it chilled until you want to serve it and have a napkin to hand to hold when pouring. Don't forget to offer guests a variety of non-alcoholic drinks.

If your party is fairly informal you can be flexible over the shape of glasses and stick to versatile Paris goblets, long-stemmed glasses with a round bowl which hold about 100 ml (3½ fl oz) of wine. However, remember that mulled wine needs special heat-resistant glasses or mugs. Frosting glasses is an imaginative way to decorate a drink – dip the rims into lightly beaten egg white, then into caster sugar. Give non-alcoholic drinks a sophisticated look with fruits on cocktail sticks and fancy straws – thread cocktail cherries, fruits and olives, etc., on to sticks several hours ahead.

Coffee or tea can be refreshing at the end of the party. A plateful of petit fours arranged on a doiley makes a delightful accompaniment – choose from Turkish delight, mini-meringues, macaroons, chocolate-dipped nuts, chocolate clusters, fudge and sugared almonds to complete your party.

Suggested Menus

COCKTAIL PARTY
FINGER BUFFET

Curried chicken choux puffs
Baby quiches
Salami cornets
Smoked salmon triangles
Taramasalata on fried croûtes
Cucumber boats with prawns
Deep fried scampi with caper sauce
Ham roulades
Asparagus rolls

Chicken and ham vol-au-vents
Bread sticks with Parma ham
Peanut sables
Stuffed raw mushrooms
Smoked salmon and crab rolls
Rollmops on pumpernickel
Cheese balls with olives
Oven hot dogs
Curried chicken eccles

Stuffed dates
Herby chicken with cucumber dip
Avocado dip
Cheese and ham fingers
Goujons of sole

WEDDING RECEPTION FINGER BUFFET

Miniature Cornish pasties
Chicken drumsticks
Mini pizzas
Cheese shells
Cocktail Scotch eggs
Tuna crescents
Cocktail sausages with mustard dip

Stuffed celery boats
Egg and bacon rolls
Caviare and cream cheese canapés
Savoury meat balls with barbecue sauce
Cheese and ale toasties
Melon balls with Parma ham
Stuffed eggs with prawns
Assorted sandwiches

FORK BUFFETS

Hawaiian chicken
Salmon with cucumber and yoghurt salad
Ham cornets with liver pâté filling
Hazelnut torte
Chocolate profiteroles

Contrefilet of beef
Chicken and vegetable terrine
York ham with peaches
Viennese curd cake with apricot sauce
Chocolate cases with ginger
Mini meringues

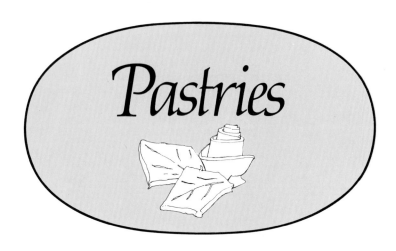

Pastries

CHEESE WHIRLS

Makes 20 whirls

225 g (8 oz) frozen puff pastry,
  thawed
3 teaspoons yeast extract

225 g (8 oz) Cheddar cheese,
  finely grated

PREPARATION TIME: 20 minutes
COOKING TIME: 15 minutes
OVEN: 220°C, 425°F, Gas Mark 7

---

1. Roll the pastry thinly to a 30 cm (12 inch) square.
2. Dot liberally with the yeast extract. Sprinkle with the cheese, saving 3-4 tablespoons for the topping.
3. Roll up the pastry carefully to make a Swiss roll shape. Using a sharp knife, cut into 20 thin slices.
4. Arrange the slices flat on a dampened baking sheet, adjusting the round shape as necessary. Sprinkle the remaining cheese on top of each whirl.
5. Bake in a preheated oven for 15 minutes. Transfer to a wire tray immediately. Serve hot or cold.

CURRIED CHICKEN CHOUX PUFFS

Makes 50

CHOUX PASTRY:
225 ml (7½ fl oz) water
75 g (3 oz) hard margarine
100 g (4 oz) plain flour
3 small eggs, beaten

CHICKEN FILLING:
40 g (1½ oz) butter
1 small onion, finely chopped
1 garlic clove, crushed

1 tablespoon curry paste
50 g (2 oz) plain flour
450 ml (¾ pint) milk
salt
freshly ground black pepper
225 g (8 oz) cooked chicken,
  finely chopped

TO GARNISH:
sprigs of parsley

PREPARATION TIME: 25 minutes
COOKING TIME: 20-25 minutes
OVEN: 220°C, 425°F, Gas Mark 7

These puffs are served cold. The addition of curry paste to the puffs gives an unusual flavour.

1.   To make the choux pastry, melt the margarine in a pan, add the water and bring to the boil.
2.   Add the flour all at once and beat until the mixture leaves the side of the pan.
3.   Cool slightly, then add the eggs a little at a time, beating well. Take care not to get the mixture too wet – it should be smooth, shiny and should hold its shape.
4.   Place the mixture in a piping bag fitted with a plain 1 cm (½ inch) nozzle and pipe small mounds the size of a walnut on to a dampened greased baking sheet.
5.   Bake in a preheated oven for 20 minutes until dark golden brown. Make a slit in the side of each puff and cool on a wire tray.
6.   To make the chicken filling, melt the butter in a pan and fry the onion and garlic until softened. Add the curry paste. Stir in the flour and cook gently for 2 minutes.
7.   Add the milk gradually, beating well, and bring to the boil, stirring constantly. Season to taste. Fold in the chicken.
8.   When cold, pipe or spoon the filling into the choux puffs. Ⓕ Serve garnished with parsley sprigs.

Ⓕ These puffs can be frozen for 2 months and take 1½ hours to thaw.

Cheese whirls; Curried chicken choux puffs

From the left: Anchovy puffs; Baby quiches

ANCHOVY PUFFS

Makes 16-18

200 ml (⅓ pint) milk
25 g (1 oz) butter
salt
90 g (3 ½ oz) plain flour
2 eggs, beaten
1 × 90 g (3 ½ oz) can anchovy
 fillets, drained,

rinsed and finely chopped

TO GARNISH:
lettuce leaves

PREPARATION TIME: 20-25 minutes
COOKING TIME: 25 minutes
OVEN: 180°C, 350°F, Gas Mark 4

---

1.   Pour the milk into a saucepan with the butter and salt to taste.
2.   Heat to boiling point, then reduce the heat and pour in the flour, stirring constantly with a wooden spoon.
3.   Remove from the heat and allow to cool slightly.
4.   Beat in the eggs a little at a time. Fold in the anchovies.
5.   Using a teaspoon, place blobs of the mixture on to a greased baking sheet and bake in a preheated oven for 25 minutes until puffed and golden brown. Ⓕ
6.   Serve warm, on a bed of lettuce leaves.

Ⓕ The anchovy puffs can be frozen for up to 2 months and can be reheated from frozen in a preheated oven for 15 minutes at 200°C, 400°F, Gas Mark 6.

BABY QUICHES

Makes 60

SHORTCRUST PASTRY:
1 kg (2 lb) plain flour, sifted
1 teaspoon salt
225 g (8 oz) margarine
225 g (8 oz) lard
12-16 tablespoons water

FILLING:
50 g (2 oz) butter
3 large onions, finely chopped
6 rashers streaky bacon,
   chopped

4 eggs, beaten
600 ml (1 pint) milk
salt
freshly ground black pepper
2 teaspoons dry mustard
175 g (6 oz) matured Cheddar
   cheese, grated
4 large tomatoes, skinned and
   roughly chopped

PREPARATION TIME: 25 minutes, plus chilling
COOKING TIME: 20 minutes, per batch
OVEN: 200°C, 400°F, Gas Mark 6

These tartlets should be served warm.

1.   Place the flour and salt in a mixing bowl. Rub in the margarine and lard until the mixture resembles fine bread-crumbs.
2.   Add enough of the water to give a firm dough. Gently knead until smooth on a floured surface, then chill, covered with greaseproof paper, for 30 minutes.
3.   Roll out the pastry on a floured surface to a thickness of 5 mm (¼ inch). Cut out rounds with a plain cutter to line patty or tartlet tins.
4.   To make the filling, melt the butter in a pan and fry the onion gently until soft and the bacon until crisp. Put a little of the mixture in the bottom of each tartlet case.
5.   In a jug mix together the eggs, milk, salt, pepper, mustard and cheese. Pour the mixture over the onion in the tartlet cases. Top each baby quiche with a small piece of bacon or tomato.
6.   Bake in a preheated oven for 20 minutes until set and golden brown.
7.   Turn out and cool slightly on a wire tray. F

F These tartlets can be frozen for up to 2 months. They can be reheated from frozen.

VARIATIONS:

Spinach and Cheese
To the fried onion, add 225 g (8 oz) finely chopped frozen spinach (thawed and drained well).

Mushroom, Bacon and Cheese
Finely chop 225 g (8 oz) mushrooms and 125 g (4 oz) streaky bacon and fry gently until soft in the 50 g (2 oz) butter with the chopped onion. Top each quiche with mushroom slices.

CHICKEN AND HAM VOL-AU-VENTS

Makes 20

1 × 450 g (1 lb) packet frozen
  puff pastry, thawed, or 20
  frozen cocktail vol-au-vent
  cases
1 egg, beaten

FILLING:
25 g (1 oz) margarine
25 g (1 oz) plain flour
½ chicken stock cube,
  crumbled

300 ml (½ pint) milk
2 tablespoons double or
  whipping cream
salt
freshly ground black pepper
175 g (6 oz) cooked ham, diced
175 g (6 oz) cold cooked
  chicken, diced

TO GARNISH:
sprigs of parsley and dill

PREPARATION TIME: 25-30 minutes
COOKING TIME: 15 minutes
OVEN: 200°C, 400°F, Gas Mark 6

1. If using frozen pastry, roll out the pastry thinly on a floured surface and cut into 20 rounds with a 7½ cm (3 inch) fluted pastry cutter. Place the rounds on a dampened baking sheet and brush with beaten egg.
2. Cut circles on the rounds with a 5 cm (2 inch) cutter, without cutting right through the pastry.
3. Bake the vol-au-vent cases in a preheated oven for 15 minutes until well risen and golden brown. Ⓕ
4. Meanwhile, make the filling. Melt the margarine in a pan, stir in the flour and stock cube and cook gently for 2 minutes, stirring constantly.
5. Remove the pan from the heat and gradually add the milk. Return the pan to the heat and bring slowly to the boil, stirring constantly until the sauce thickens. Allow the sauce to go cold, then add the cream, salt and pepper, ham and cold chicken and stir to mix thoroughly. Ⓕ
6. When cooked, remove the vol-au-vent cases from the oven and leave to cool. Lift the tops with a pointed knife and reserve. Press the centre of the vol-au-vent cases down to make room for the filling.
7. Using a teaspoon, fill each vol-au-vent case with the filling and replace the reserved tops. Garnish with parsley and dill and serve warm.

Ⓕ Both cases and filling can be frozen separately for up to 2 months. Thaw for 30 minutes at room temperature.

VARIATIONS:

Egg and Prawn
Omit the ham and chicken and add 225 g (8 oz) peeled prawns and 4 hard-boiled eggs, roughly chopped, to the basic sauce.

Curry and Mushroom
Again, omit the ham and chicken and add 450 g (1 lb) button mushrooms, finely chopped and fried gently in 50 g (2 oz) butter and 1 dessertspoon curry powder to the basic sauce.

Chicken and ham vol-au-vents; Cheese and ham fingers

CHEESE AND HAM FINGERS

Makes 14

1 × 225 g (8 oz) packet frozen
  puff pastry, thawed
1 teaspoon made mustard
100 g (4 oz) Cheddar cheese,
  grated

100 g (4 oz) cooked ham, finely
  chopped
freshly ground black pepper
1 egg, beaten

PREPARATION TIME: 25-30 minutes
COOKING TIME: 40-45 minutes
OVEN: 220°C, 425°F, Gas Mark 7
then 190°C, 375°F, Gas Mark 5

1. Cut the pastry in half and roll out each piece on a floured surface to make strips measuring 30 × 18 cm (12 × 7 inches).
2. Place 1 strip on a dampened baking sheet. Spread with the mustard, then with the cheese and ham, leaving a 1 cm (½ inch) margin all round the edge. Sprinkle with pepper.
3. Moisten the pastry edges with water, place the second strip of pastry on top and press firmly to seal. Brush with beaten egg and cut across into thin fingers, separating them slightly.
4. Bake in a preheated oven for 15 minutes, reduce the heat and cook for a further 25-30 minutes. Ⓕ Serve hot.

Ⓕ The cheese and ham fingers can be frozen for up to 2 months. Thaw for 2 hours.

CAVIAR AND CREAM CHEESE CANAPÉS

Makes 25-30

1 × 225 g (8 oz) packet frozen
   shortcrust pastry, thawed
225 g (8 oz) full fat soft cheese
1 tablespoon single cream
1 teaspoon sherry
1 teaspoon brandy
1 teaspoon lemon juice
few drops of Tabasco sauce

salt
freshly ground black pepper

TO GARNISH:
lemon twists
caviar or mock caviar
fresh tarragon leaves
   (optional)

PREPARATION TIME: 25 minutes
COOKING TIME: 12-15 minutes
OVEN: 200°C, 400°F, Gas Mark 6

It is a good idea to vary shapes when making pastry canapés as the presentation will then look particularly good.

1. Roll out the pastry thinly on a floured surface. Cut the pastry into shapes with a variety of small fluted cutters.
2. Place the shapes on a greased baking sheet and bake in a preheated oven for 12-15 minutes, until golden brown. Cool on a wire rack. ⅋
3. Mix the cheese in a bowl with the cream, sherry, brandy, lemon juice, Tabasco and salt and pepper.
4. Put the mixture in a piping bag fitted with a star nozzle and pipe on to the pastry shapes.
5. To serve, garnish with lemon, caviar and tarragon leaves, if liked.

⅋ The pastry shapes can be frozen for up to 2 months. Thaw for 1 hour at room temperature.

PEANUT SABLÉS

Makes 60

175 g (6 oz) butter
175 g (6 oz) plain flour, sifted
175 g (6 oz) Cheddar cheese,
  grated
salt

freshly ground black pepper
1 egg, beaten, to glaze
100 g (4 oz) salted peanuts,
  coarsely chopped

PREPARATION TIME: 20-30 minutes
COOKING TIME: 10 minutes, or until golden brown
OVEN: 190°C, 375°F, Gas Mark 5

These sablés are mouthwatering served cold. They can be made in advance and kept in an airtight container for 1 week.

1.   In a mixing bowl rub the fat into the flour until the mixture resembles fine breadcrumbs. Add the cheese and the salt and pepper and knead together to make a dough.
2.   Roll out the dough thinly and cut into strips 5 cm (2 inches) wide.
3.   Brush with beaten egg, sprinkle with peanuts and cut each strip into triangles.
4.   Place the triangles on a baking sheet lined with grease-proof paper. (Cheese scorches easily, so you can lift the greaseproof paper off the baking sheet as soon as the triangles come out of the oven, to prevent further cooking.)
5.   Bake in a preheated oven for 10-15 minutes until golden brown.
6.   Cool on a wire tray. ⒡ Serve cold.

⒡ The sablés can be frozen for up to 2 months. Pack very carefully in a rigid box, interleaved with plastic tissue or soft paper. Thaw for 1 hour at room temperature.

CURRIED CHICKEN ECCLES

Makes 16

FILLING:
12 g (½ oz) butter, melted
1 small onion, finely chopped
1 dessertspoon curry powder
1 dessertspoon plain flour
1 tablespoon Worcestershire
    sauce
2 tablespoons pineapple juice
1 tablespoon lemon juice

2 tablespoons water or stock
100 g (4 oz) cold cooked
    chicken, finely chopped
1 ring canned pineapple,
    finely chopped
25 g (1 oz) sultanas
225 g (8 oz) frozen puff pastry,
    thawed
1 egg, beaten

PREPARATION TIME: 30 minutes
COOKING TIME: 15-20 minutes
OVEN: 220°C, 425°F, Gas Mark 7

1.   Melt the butter in a pan, add the onion and fry gently for 3 minutes until the onion is transparent.
2.   Add the curry powder and flour and cook for 2 minutes, stirring constantly.
3.   Add all the liquids slowly, stirring well. Bring to the boil and simmer for 3 minutes. Leave to go cold, then add the chicken, pineapple and sultanas.
4.   Roll out the pastry very thinly on a lightly floured board.
5.   Cut sixteen 7½ cm (3 inch) rounds with a plain cutter, re-rolling the pastry if necessary. Be careful to retain the puff pastry layers.
6.   Divide the filling evenly between the pastry rounds, leaving the edges clear. Dampen the edges of the pastry with water and gather them together to seal.
7.   Turn the pastry circles over so that the smooth side is on top and roll lightly to flatten and form 'Eccles cakes'.
8.   Make 3 slits in the top of each 'cake' and brush well with beaten egg.
9.   Place the 'cakes' on a greased baking sheet and chill in the refrigerator for 30 minutes.
10.   Bake near the top of a preheated oven for 15-20 minutes.
🄵 Serve hot or cold, garnished with cress, if liked.

🄵 The chicken eccles can be frozen for up to 2 months. Thaw for 1½-2 hours at room temperature.

Centre: Curried chicken eccles; *Outside:* Tuna crescents

TUNA CRESCENTS

Makes 20-24

FILLING:
1 tablespoon oil
1 onion, finely chopped
½ medium green pepper, de-
  seeded and cut in tiny cubes
1 × 200 g (7 oz) can tuna in oil,
  drained and flaked
1 hard-boiled egg, finely
  chopped

2 tablespoons tomato ketchup
salt
freshly ground black pepper
pinch of nutmeg
1 tablespoon parsley, finely
  chopped
450 g (1 lb) frozen puff pastry,
  thawed
oil, for deep frying

PREPARATION TIME: 30 minutes
COOKING TIME: 6-8 minutes

The crescents can be kept hot in a very low oven for up to 30 minutes.

1. Fry the onion and green pepper in heated oil until soft.
2. Mix the tuna with the egg and add the onion mixture, the tomato ketchup, salt, pepper, nutmeg and parsley.
3. Roll out the pastry on a floured surface and cut into 20-24 rounds with a 7.5 cm (3 inch) plain cutter.
4. Divide the filling between the rounds, then brush the edges with water and fold the pastry over into a crescent shape, sealing the edges very firmly.
5. Heat the oil to 180°-190°C/350°-375°F or until a cube of bread browns in 30 seconds.
6. Using a slotted spoon, lower the crescents into the oil, a few at a time, and cook until golden brown and crisp.
7. Drain the crescents on paper towels and serve on a bed of lettuce, garnished with cress, if liked.

Above: Samosas; *Below:* Spinach cheese puffs

SAMOSAS

Serves 8

DOUGH:
225 g (8 oz) plain or
   wholewheat flour
2 teaspoons baking powder
1 teaspoon salt
3 tablespoons sunflower or
   vegetable oil
150 ml (5 fl oz) water

FILLING:
1 tablespoon oil

1 onion, finely chopped
100 g (4 oz) mushrooms,
   chopped
2 teaspoons cinnamon
1 teaspoon cumin
2 teaspoons turmeric
4 tablespoons peas, cooked
oil, for deep frying

TO GARNISH:
sprigs of parsley or coriander

PREPARATION TIME: 50 minutes
COOKING TIME: 30 minutes

These triangles are delicious for those who like a spicy vegetarian pastry. Any leftover vegetables can be used instead of the peas.

1.   To make the dough, mix the flour, baking powder and salt in a bowl. Mix in the oil and water, a little at a time, until a firm dough is formed, which leaves the sides of the bowl clean.
2.   On a floured board, knead the dough with the palm of your hand for 5-8 minutes until smooth.
3.   Form the dough into a ball, brush with a little oil, then cover and set on one side while you make the filling.
4.   To make the filling, heat the oil in a frying pan and cook the onion until softened. Add the mushrooms and cook for 2

---

minutes. Add the dry spices and peas (or other vegetables) and cook for a further 2 minutes. Allow the mixture to cool.
5. Divide the dough into 8 equal pieces. Form the pieces into balls, flatten them and roll out thinly on a floured surface to make circles 10 cm (4 inches) in diameter.
6. Cut the circles in half with a sharp knife. Moisten half the cut edge of each semi-circle, fold in half and press the cut edge over to seal and to form a wide cone.
7. Cup each cone open in your hand and spoon in enough filling to make three-quarters full. Dampen the edges and press over to seal completely.
8. Heat the oil to 180°-190°C/350°-375°F, or until a cube of bread browns in 30 seconds. Deep fry the samosas in batches for 3-4 minutes until golden brown. Remove with a slotted spoon and drain on paper towels.
9. Serve immediately, garnished with parsley or coriander and with plenty of paper napkins to hand.

SPINACH CHEESE PUFFS

Makes 40

FILLING:
225 g (8 oz) Feta or goat's cheese
175 g (6 oz) curd cheese
3 tablespoons olive oil
40 g (1½ oz) finely chopped parsley
1 teaspoon nutmeg, grated
freshly ground black pepper
3 eggs, beaten

450 g (1 lb) spinach, cooked, drained and finely chopped
225 g (8 oz) phyllo pastry sheets, at room temperature
100 g (4 oz) unsalted butter, melted

PREPARATION TIME: 2 hours
COOKING TIME: 12-14 minutes
OVEN: 220°C, 425°F, Gas Mark 7

These puffs make a very appetizing warm snack.

1. To make the filling, rinse the Feta cheese under cold water, drain and crumble into a bowl. Blend in the curd cheese, olive oil, parsley, nutmeg and seasoning. Add the beaten eggs and mix well, then add the cooked spinach.
2. Cut the sheets of phyllo into quarters cross-wise. Brush each quarter sheet, as you use it, with warm, melted butter. Place 1 teaspoon of spinach mixture 2.5 cm (1 inch) from the bottom edge of the sheet, fold the bottom up over the filling, then fold the sides in towards the middle. Brush with warm melted butter and roll the sheet loosely. Repeat until all the ingredients are used up.
3. Place the rolls seam-side down on a baking sheet and brush with warm, melted butter. Do not allow the puffs to touch as they will expand during cooking.
4. Bake the puffs in a preheated oven for 12-14 minutes until plump, crisp and golden. Serve on an attractive dish.

BRISLING ENVELOPES

Makes 12

SHORTCRUST PASTRY:
225 g (8 oz) plain flour
salt
100 g (4 oz) lard and hard
  margarine, mixed
4 tablespoons water

2 × 90 g (3½ oz) cans brisling
  or sild

TO GLAZE:
beaten egg

TO GARNISH:
curly endive leaves

PREPARATION TIME: 20 minutes
COOKING TIME: 30 minutes
OVEN: 190°C, 375°F, Gas Mark 5

Brislings are small fish, rather like sardines.

1. Sieve the plain flour and salt into a mixing bowl. Rub in the fat until the mixture resembles fine breadcrumbs. Add sufficient water to form a firm dough.
2. On a floured surface, roll out to a rectangular shape and cut into twelve 5 cm (2 inch) squares.
3. Lay the brisling diagonally across the squares and dampen the edges with beaten egg. Fold the 4 corners of the pastry to meet in the middle. ⨎
4. Brush the envelopes with beaten egg and place on a greased baking sheet. Bake in a preheated oven for 30 minutes until golden brown.
5. Serve warm, garnished with curly endive leaves.

⨎ The envelopes can be frozen for up to 2 months. Thaw for 1 hour at room temperature.

HOT LIVER PÂTÉ

Serves 8

175 g (6 oz) butter
1 onion, peeled and chopped
225 g (8 oz) chicken livers,
  coarsely chopped
4 teaspoons Worcestershire
  sauce

4 teaspoons Dijon mustard
300 ml (½ pint) single cream
large pinch of cayenne pepper
6 tablespoons white
  breadcrumbs
lettuce leaves, to garnish

PREPARATION TIME: 20 minutes
COOKING TIME: 15-20 minutes
OVEN: 190°C, 375°F, Gas Mark 5

This savoury pâté is excellent served with hot toast.

1. Melt 100 g (4 oz) of the butter in a frying pan and fry the onion until soft. Add the chicken livers and fry for a further 2-3 minutes.
2. Remove from the heat and add the Worcestershire sauce, Dijon mustard, cream and cayenne pepper.
3. Divide the mixture between 8 individual ramekin dishes or 1 large serving dish. Sprinkle the top with breadcrumbs.
4. Melt the remaining butter and pour over the pâté.
5. Bake in a preheated oven for 15-20 minutes. Serve immediately, garnished with lettuce leaves.

TERRINE DE CANARD AUX RAISINS DE CORINTHE

Serves 16 (Makes 2)

1 ½ kg (3 ½ lb) duck
450 g (1 lb) belly pork
175 g (6 oz) currants
175 ml (6 fl oz) Grand Marnier
*225 g (8 oz) stewing veal, cut
    into 2.5 cm (1 inch) cubes*
*liver from the duck, plus 1 or 2
    chicken livers*
2 eggs, beaten
salt

freshly ground black pepper
*225 g (8 oz) streaky, unsmoked
    bacon, rind removed*
2 bay leaves
2 sprigs thyme
grated rind of 1 orange

TO GARNISH:
1 lettuce, shredded

PREPARATION TIME: 1½ hours, plus cooling and chilling
overnight
COOKING TIME: 3½ hours, including roasting duck
OVEN: 160°C, 325°F, Gas Mark 3

The terrines are made the day before and chilled overnight.

1.   Roast the duck together with the belly pork, removing the pork after 1 hour. Cook the duck for a further 30 minutes.
2.   While the duck is cooking and cooling, soak the currants in half of the Grand Marnier.
3.   When the duck has cooled completely, remove the breast fillets carefully with a sharp knife and marinate in the rest of the Grand Marnier.
4.   Strip the remaining flesh from the duck, discarding the skin. Cut the pork into 2.5 cm (1 inch) cubes. Place the duck trimmings, pork and uncooked veal and livers in a food processor, a half quantity at a time, and mince. Add the currants and their marinade, the eggs and salt and pepper and mix thoroughly.
5.   Line 2 medium terrines with pieces of bacon and half-fill each one with a quarter of the meat mixture.
6.   Remove the duck breasts from their marinade and slice horizontally into 2 pieces.
7.   Place the 2 halves in a layer in each terrine, then cover with the rest of the meat mixture.
8.   Divide the remaining marinade between the 2 terrines and top each with a bay leaf and a sprig of thyme. Cover with well-buttered greaseproof paper and a lid or foil.
9.   Place the terrines in a bain-marie in a preheated oven and cook slowly for 2 hours. Allow to cool before removing the lids. Press with a weight and chill overnight. [F]
10.   Slice and serve on a bed of shredded lettuce.

[F] The terrines can be frozen for up to 2 months. Thaw for 4-5 hours at room temperature.

From the left: Farmhouse pâté; Terrine de canard aux raisins

FARMHOUSE PÂTÉ

Serves 6

450 g (1 lb) pig's liver, minced
175 g (6 oz) belly of fresh pork,
  minced
50 g (2 oz) streaky bacon, cut
  into small strips
salt
freshly ground black pepper

½ clove garlic, finely chopped
1 tablespoon white wine
1 tablespoon brandy

TO GARNISH:
leaves of celery

PREPARATION TIME: 25 minutes, plus 2 days' chilling
COOKING TIME: 1 hour 15 minutes
OVEN: 160°C, 325°F, Gas Mark 3

The farmhouse pâté should be made 48 hours before it is required to allow the flavours to mature and blend together. It is delicious served with toast or French bread.

1. Place the pig's liver and pork in a bowl and mix together thoroughly.
2. Add the salt and pepper, garlic, wine and brandy.
3. Press the mixture into a 450 g (1 lb) terrine, arranging the strips of streaky bacon in a criss-cross pattern across the top.
4. Stand in a roasting pan half filled with hot water. Cover the terrine with foil and cook in a preheated oven for 1 hour. Remove the foil and cook for a further 15 minutes.
5. Leave until cold. F Cover with a weight and refrigerate for 48 hours. Serve cold with bread and butter.

F The pâté can be frozen for up to 2 months. Thaw at room temperature for 3-4 hours.

COUNTRY TERRINE OF VEGETABLES

Serves 6

120 ml (4 fl oz) groundnut oil
225 g (8 oz) cauliflower,
  divided into florets
100 g (4 oz) onion, peeled and
  chopped
75 g (3 oz) carrot, peeled and
  chopped
1 green pepper, cored, seeded
  and chopped
1 red pepper, cored, seeded
  and chopped
225 g (8 oz) potato, cut into
  small cubes
pinch of ginger
pinch of mace

pinch of turmeric
pinch of paprika
50 g (2 oz) tomato purée
600 ml (1 pint) water
225 g (8 oz) broccoli
grated rind of 1 lemon
4 tablespoons lemon juice
2 garlic cloves, peeled
150 g (5 oz) curd cheese
4 eggs, beaten
salt
freshly ground black pepper
50 g (2 oz) Parmesan cheese,
  grated

PREPARATION TIME: 25 minutes
COOKING TIME: 50 minutes
OVEN: 200°C, 400°F, Gas Mark 6

This decorative, coarse-textured vegetable terrine makes a good accompaniment to cold buffets. In order to make the most of its fresh ingredients, serve it no later than on the day after it is made.

1. Fry the cauliflower, onion, carrot, peppers and potato gently in oil for 5 minutes. Add spices and tomato purée.
2. Pour on the water and boil for 20 minutes, then drain, reserving the liquid for boiling the broccoli for 10 minutes.
3. Drain the cooking liquid, pour into a blender with the lemon rind, juice, garlic and curd cheese, and purée.

---

4. Combine the cheese purée and cauliflower mixture, add eggs and season. Chop the broccoli roughly and stir into mixture. Turn into a terrine and sprinkle with Parmesan. Bake for 50 minutes. Cool and serve with hot toast.

CHICKEN AND VEGETABLE TERRINE

Serves 6 or 12 as an appetizer

3 boneless chicken breasts,
    1 kg (2 lb) total weight
450 ml (15 fl oz) double cream,
    chilled
salt
freshly ground black pepper
1 bunch watercress, finely
    chopped
100 g (4 oz) small new carrots
100 g (4 oz) French beans

100 g (4 oz) courgettes
25 g (1 oz) butter
75 g (3 oz) small button
    mushrooms
butter, for greasing
100 g (4 oz) canned artichoke
    bases, drained

TO GARNISH:
1 carrot, finely grated

PREPARATION TIME: 1 hour 20 minutes, plus chilling
COOKING TIME: 1 hour
OVEN: 170°C, 325°F, Gas Mark 3

1. Cut up the chicken and mince or process finely. Mix with the cream, season and chill. In a separate bowl mix the watercress with one-third of the chicken mixture. Cover both bowls of chicken stuffing and refrigerate for 2 hours.
2. Cut the carrots into neat matchstick-shaped pieces, 2.5 cm (1 inch) by 2.5 mm (⅛ inch). Cut the beans into similar pieces. Blanch the carrots and beans in separate pans of boiling, salted water for 2 minutes. Drain thoroughly.
3. Cut the courgettes into thin slices and sauté in 25 g (1 oz) of butter until golden but still quite firm. Drain thoroughly.
4. Cut the mushrooms into slices 5 mm (¼ inch) thick and then into 5 mm (¼ inch) dice.
5. Butter a 1.2 litre (2 pint) terrine dish. Spread half the watercress stuffing evenly over the base of the terrine. Arrange the carrots in neat diagonal lines over this, then spread one quarter of the chicken stuffing over the carrots.
6. Layer the courgettes with another thin layer of chicken stuffing on top. Place the mushrooms on top in diagonal lines and top with the rest of the watercress stuffing. Layer the artichoke bases, cover with stuffing, arrange the beans in diagonal lines and finish with the remaining stuffing.
7. Place a double sheet of buttered greaseproof paper over the dish and cover tightly. Place the terrine in a roasting tin with water to come half-way up the side of the dish. Bake until the mixture is just firm to the touch, about 1 hour.
8. Allow to cool a little, then drain off any juices and invert on to a serving plate. Refrigerate for 1 hour before serving.
9. Serve garnished with finely grated carrot.

From the left: Country terrine of vegetables; Chicken and vegetable terrine

MACKEREL PÂTÉ

Serves 6

200 g (7 oz) smoked mackerel
  fillets, skinned
1 tablespoon soured cream
25 g (1 oz) fresh breadcrumbs
1 tablespoon lemon juice

2 teaspoons horseradish sauce
freshly ground black pepper
lemon slices, to garnish
celery leaves, to garnish

PREPARATION TIME: 15 minutes, plus chilling

---

1. Put the smoked mackerel, soured cream, breadcrumbs, lemon juice, horseradish sauce and pepper in a mixing bowl or electric blender and mix until smooth.
2. Chill for several hours, well covered. Ⓕ
3. Garnish and serve with toasted bread.

Ⓕ The mackerel pâté can be frozen for up to 1 month. Thaw for 3 hours at room temperature or in the refrigerator overnight.

Mackerel pâté; Tuna fish mousse

TUNA FISH MOUSSE

Serves 8

3 teaspoons gelatine
1 × 415 g (14 ½ oz) can beef consommé
2 × 200 g (7 oz) cans tuna fish, drained and flaked
3 ripe tomatoes, peeled and chopped
6 hard-boiled eggs, roughly chopped
300 ml (½ pint) double or whipping cream, whipped to hold its shape
1 tablespoon lemon juice
1 teaspoon Worcestershire sauce
salt
freshly ground black pepper
1 tablespoon chopped chives
1 tablespoon chopped parsley
sprig of parsley, to garnish

PREPARATION TIME: 15 minutes, plus chilling overnight

1.   In a bowl over a pan of hot water, dissolve the gelatine in the consommé and leave to cool.
2.   Place the tuna fish, tomatoes and egg in a large bowl. Add the cooled beef consommé, the cream, lemon juice, Worcestershire sauce, salt and pepper. Stir in the herbs.
3.   Pour the mixture into a lightly oiled 1.25 litre (2 pint) mould, cover and refrigerate overnight.
4.   Turn out on to a serving plate. Garnish and serve with a salad and hot toast.

Bread

SMOKED SALMON TRIANGLES

Makes 64

8 slices brown bread, crusts
   removed
50 g (2 oz) butter, softened
225 g (8 oz) smoked salmon,
   very thinly sliced

freshly ground black pepper
lemon juice

TO GARNISH:
1 lemon, cut into wedges

PREPARATION TIME: 20 minutes

---

1.   Spread the bread with butter. Cover each slice with smoked salmon and sprinkle with pepper and lemon juice.
2.   Cut the slices into 8 triangles. A F Garnish and serve.

A The triangles can be made 1 day in advance and refrigerated.
F The triangles can be frozen for up to 1 month. Thaw for 40 minutes at room temperature.

FINGER ROLLS WITH VARIOUS TOPPINGS

Makes 24 open rolls

12 finger rolls, halved
75 g (3 oz) butter

TO GARNISH:
stuffed olives, sliced

lemon slices, quartered
cucumber slices, quartered
thin slices of radish

PREPARATION TIME: 20 minutes

TOPPINGS:

Cream Cheese and Pineapple
225 g (8 oz) full fat soft cheese
1 × 215 g (7 ½ oz) can crushed pineapple, drained
1 tablespoon mayonnaise

Tuna Fish and Mayonnaise
1 × 200 g (7 oz) can tuna in oil, drained and flaked
3 tablespoons mayonnaise
1 dessertspoon lemon juice
salt
freshly ground black pepper

These are always popular at parties and can be prepared the day before and covered with cling film. Your local baker will make small cocktail-size finger rolls if given plenty of notice. The rolls, without the topping, can be frozen for up to 2 months.

1. Cut the finger rolls in half and spread thinly with butter.
2. Mix together the ingredients for the chosen topping and spread on the rolls. Serve garnished with the olive, lemon, cucumber and radish slices.

Smoked salmon triangles; Finger rolls with various toppings

SANDWICHES
(VARIOUS FILLINGS)

Makes 44

1 white sliced loaf	*salt*
100 g (4 oz) butter, softened	*freshly ground black pepper*
5 hard-boiled eggs, mashed	*2 punnets mustard and cress*
3-4 tablespoons mayonnaise	

PREPARATION TIME: 20 minutes

Sandwiches can be frozen for 2 months and take approximately 1 hour to thaw. Do not freeze hard-boiled egg or salad fillings. They will keep really well in the refrigerator for 1 day covered in cling film. To cut even sandwiches and remove the crusts, it is a good idea to pile several on top of each other and then cut through the pile.

1.   Spread each slice of bread thinly with butter.
2.   Mash the eggs and mayonnaise together, adding salt and pepper to taste.
3.   Spread the mixture on to the bread, with a sprinkling of mustard and cress, then cover with another slice of bread.
4.   Cut the sandwiches into 4 squares.

Various fillings
(for 1 large sliced loaf)

Liver Pâté and Tomato with Brown Bread

350 g (12 oz) spreading pâté
225 g (8 oz) tomatoes, thinly sliced
salt
freshly ground black pepper
mustard and cress, to garnish

Avocado Pear and Prawns with White Bread

4 ripe avocados, thinly sliced and dipped in lemon juice
350 g (12 oz) prawns
4 tablespoons mayonnaise
sprigs of dill, to garnish

Salmon and Cucumber with Brown Bread

1 × 225 g (8 oz) can red salmon, drained and flaked, with 2-3 tablespoons mayonnaise
½ cucumber, skinned and thinly sliced
salt
freshly ground black pepper

Clockwise from bottom, left: Avocado pear and prawns with white bread; Salmon and cucumber with brown bread; Liver pâté and tomato with brown bread; Egg and cress with white bread

HAM ROULADES

Makes 60

6 slices cooked ham
175 g (6 oz) full fat soft cheese
10 slices brown bread,

buttered and crusts
removed

PREPARATION TIME: 20-25 minutes, plus chilling

Use square-cut ham, usually shoulder.

1. Spread the ham slices thickly and evenly with the soft cheese.
2. Roll up into a sausage shape and, using a sharp knife, cut into 10 pinwheels.
3. Cut each slice of bread into 6 small squares.
4. Lay each pinwheel on a square of bread and serve after chilling for 30 minutes. F

F The roulades freeze well for up to 2 months. Thaw for 40 minutes at room temperature.

TARAMASALATA ON FRIED CROÛTES

Makes 40

225 g (8 oz) smoked cod's roe,
   skin removed, soaked
   overnight
1 garlic clove, finely chopped
175 g (6 oz) fresh breadcrumbs
2 tablespoons milk
8 tablespoons oil

2 tablespoons lemon juice
freshly ground black pepper
fried croûtes (page 53)

TO GARNISH:
sprigs of dill

PREPARATION TIME: 20-25 minutes

Taramasalata can be made about 1 week in advance of a party and kept refrigerated in an airtight container.

1. Place the cod's roe in a mixing bowl. Add the garlic and beat well until smooth.
2. Soak the bread in the milk for 3 minutes, then squeeze to remove as much milk as possible.
3. Add the soaked bread to the cod's roe and then add the oil, a little at a time, mixing thoroughly. The mixture should be of a piping consistency. Add the lemon juice and pepper.
4. Place the mixture in a piping bag fitted with a 1 cm (½ inch) plain nozzle and pipe on to the fried croûtes. Serve garnished with dill sprigs.

ASPARAGUS ROLLS

Makes 60 small rolls

1 large sliced brown loaf,
   crusts removed
175 g (6 oz) butter

1 × 350 g (12 oz) can
   asparagus tips, drained

PREPARATION TIME: 20-25 minutes, plus chilling

---

1. Using a rolling pin, roll the slices of bread until very thin.
2. Butter a slice of bread and lay asparagus tips along the long edges. Roll up and place join-side down on a tray.
3. Repeat for all slices of bread, packing the rolls tightly together to stop them unrolling. Ⓐ Refrigerate for 1 hour.
4. When ready to serve, cut each roll into 3, garnish with more asparagus tips and arrange on a serving dish.

Ⓐ The asparagus rolls can be made the day before, covered with cling film and refrigerated.

From the top: Asparagus rolls; Taramasalata on fried croûtes; Ham roulades

SKORDALIA

Serves 8

4 large garlic cloves, peeled
    and crushed
1 egg yolk
salt
freshly ground black pepper
150 ml (¼ pint) olive oil

50 g (2 oz) fresh white
    breadcrumbs
50 g (2 oz) ground almonds
1 tablespoon lemon juice
1 tablespoon chopped parsley
fried croûtes (page 53)

PREPARATION TIME: 15 minutes

If Skordalia is made in larger quantities it can be prepared in
an electric blender or food processor. If the mixture curdles,
add the mixture gradually to a fresh egg yolk. Serve with
hard-boiled eggs, olives, parsley and quartered tomatoes.

1.   Mix the garlic with the egg yolk and seasoning. Add the
oil a drop at a time until the mixture thickens, then add the
remaining oil a little more quickly.
2.   Add the breadcrumbs, ground almonds, lemon juice and
parsley and mix thoroughly.
3.   Spread the mixture on to fried croûtes.

MINI PIZZAS

Makes 30

1 × 500 g (1¼ lb) packet
    white bread mix
3 tablespoons oil
2 onions, finely chopped
2 cloves garlic, crushed
1 × 750 g (1¾ lb) can
    tomatoes
2 tablespoons tomato purée
2 teaspoons dried mixed herbs
2 teaspoons sugar
salt
freshly ground black pepper

25 g (1 oz) Parmesan cheese,
    grated
100 g (4 oz) cooked ham,
    chopped
100 g (4 oz) salami, chopped
1 × 50 g (2 oz) can anchovy
    fillets, drained and chopped
50 g (2 oz) black olives, stoned
    and sliced
100 g (4 oz) Cheddar cheese,
    grated
chopped parsley

PREPARATION TIME: 40 minutes, plus rising
COOKING TIME: 15-20 minutes per batch
OVEN: 220°C, 425°F, Gas Mark 7
then 230°C, 450°F, Gas Mark 8

1.   Make up the bread mix according to the packet
instructions and leave to rise.
2.   Heat 2 tablespoons of the oil in a frying pan, add the
onions and garlic and fry gently until soft.

Top: Mini pizzas; *Bottom:* Skordalia

3.   Add the tomatoes with their juice, the tomato purée, herbs, sugar, salt and pepper. Simmer until the mixture thickens.
4.   Roll out the bread dough to a thickness of 5 mm (¼ inch) and cut into 6 cm (2½ inch) rounds with a plain cutter.
5.   Place the dough circles on greased baking sheets. Brush each circle with the remaining oil and sprinkle with the Parmesan cheese. Top with the tomato mixture.
6.   Bake in a preheated oven for 10-15 minutes until risen and golden brown.
7.   Mix together the ham, salami and anchovy fillets and divide the mixture between the pizzas. Place an olive slice in the centre of each pizza and sprinkle with grated cheese. Return to the oven for 5 minutes.
8.   Sprinkle the mini pizzas with chopped parsley and serve hot or cold.

TOASTED BREAD AND GARLIC

Makes 32 squares

2 garlic cloves, peeled
1 dried red chilli pepper
salt
freshly ground black pepper

2 tablespoons lemon juice
40 g (1½ oz) butter, softened
4 slices white bread

PREPARATION TIME: 10-15 minutes
COOKING TIME: 20 minutes
OVEN: 200°C, 400°F, Gas Mark 6

These are delicious served on their own in pretty, small dishes. They do not freeze but can be prepared the day before and baked on the day of the party.

1. Pound the garlic and chilli with a pestle and mortar, adding the salt and pepper to taste.
2. Stir in the lemon juice, then mix in the butter.
3. Spread the mixture on the slices of bread and place on a baking sheet. Bake in a preheated oven for 20 minutes, until brown.
4. Remove the crusts from the bread and cut each slice into eight 2.5 cm (1 inch) squares. Serve immediately.

SCRAMBLED EGG AND CHIVES ON FRIED CROÛTES

Makes 12

4 eggs
salt
freshly ground black pepper
40 g (1½ oz) butter
4 tablespoons mayonnaise
2 tablespoons finely chopped

chives
12 fried croûtes (page 53)

TO GARNISH:
12 small green grapes
12 small black grapes

PREPARATION TIME: 20 minutes
COOKING TIME: 4-5 minutes

The scrambled egg mixture can be prepared 1 day in advance, but do not assemble until just before serving.

1. Beat the eggs in a bowl with salt and pepper.
2. Melt the butter in a pan and add the beaten egg. Cook, stirring, over a low heat until the mixture is light and fluffy.
3. Allow to cool, then stir in the mayonnaise and chives.
4. Top each croûte with a little of the scrambled egg mixture and garnish with the green and black grapes.

FRIED CROÛTES

6 slices of bread
oil, for deep frying

These are very crunchy and will keep for 3 months in an airtight container in the freezer.

1.   Remove the crusts from the bread and cut into 5 cm (2 inch) squares, using a very sharp knife.
2.   Heat the oil to 180°-190°/350°-375°F or until a cube of bread browns in 30 seconds. Lower the bread squares into the oil and toss them frequently until golden brown.
3.   Lift out on to paper towels to drain and leave to cool.
4.   Pack into an airtight container, if storing.

Top: Toasted bread and garlic; *Bottom:* Scrambled egg and chives on fried croûtes

CHEESE AND ALE TOASTIES

Makes 12

6 slices bread
75 g (3 oz) Cheddar cheese,
   grated
1 medium cooking apple,
   peeled and grated
1 medium onion, peeled and

   grated
1 teaspoon made mustard
salt
freshly ground black pepper
2-3 tablespoons ale

PREPARATION TIME: 15 minutes

The crusts are left on for toasting, to prevent burning.

1. Toast the bread with the crusts on, on one side only.
2. Mix together the cheese, apple, onion, mustard and salt and pepper and ale. Ⓐ Pile the mixture on the uncooked sides of the slices of toast and spread to the edges.
3. Place the toasties under a hot grill until light brown.
4. Remove the crusts and cut in two diagonally. Serve hot.

Ⓐ The mixture can be prepared 2-3 hours before the party.

Clockwise from the top: Bread tartlet cases with suggested fillings; Cheese and ale toasties; Bread sticks with parma ham

---

BREAD TARTLET CASES WITH SUGGESTED FILLINGS

Makes 20

*20 thin slices bread,
crusts removed*

100 g (4 oz) soft margarine

PREPARATION TIME: 20 minutes
COOKING TIME: 25-30 minutes
OVEN: 180°C, 350°F, Gas Mark 4

Bread tartlet cases are a good alternative to pastry for a party. They will keep in an airtight container for 1 week.

1.   Using a rolling pin, roll out the bread slices until thin.
2.   Cut out circles of bread using a 7½ cm (3 inch) round plain cutter.
3.   Spread both sides of the bread with the margarine and place in patty tins.
4.   Bake the bread cases in a preheated oven for 25-30 minutes until crisp and golden brown.
5.   Fill as required and serve hot or cold.

Suggested Fillings:
Add the following instead of the chicken and ham, to the basic sauce for vol-au-vents, page 28.

Tuna and Caper
*1 × 200 g (7 oz) can tuna,
  drained and flaked
1 teaspoon lemon juice
2 teaspoons capers, chopped
1 teaspoon chopped chives*

Asparagus and Blue Cheese
*1 × 300 g (11 oz) can
  asparagus tips, drained and
  chopped
1 teaspoon lemon juice
100 g (4 oz) blue cheese,
  crumbled*

BREAD STICKS WITH PARMA HAM

Makes 24

*100 g (4 oz) Parma ham
1 × 135 g (4¾ oz) packet
  bread sticks (Grissini)*

*TO GARNISH:
black olives
lamb's lettuce leaves*

PREPARATION TIME: 15 minutes

1.   Halve the bread sticks and cut the Parma ham into pieces big enough to wrap around the end of the sticks twice.
2.   Serve garnished with black olives and lamb's lettuce leaves.

OVEN HOT DOGS

Makes 12

12 thin slices white bread
75 g (3 oz) soft margarine
ready-made mustard

12 rashers of streaky bacon,
 rind removed
12 skinless sausages

PREPARATION TIME: 15 minutes
COOKING TIME: 20 minutes
OVEN: 200°C, 400°F, Gas Mark 6

These hot dogs make a very substantial snack. You can vary the fillings; children love tomato ketchup as a substitute for the mustard, or horseradish sauce.

1.   Cut the crusts from each slice of bread and roll out the slices with a rolling pin until thin and even.
2.   Spread 1 side of bread with margarine and a little mustard. Stretch the bacon with a palette knife until thin and place this on the slice of bread.
3.   Put the sausage at one end of the bread, then roll up firmly like a Swiss roll, securing with a cocktail stick.
4.   Spread a little more margarine on the top of the roll and place on a baking sheet.
5.   Bake in a preheated oven for 20 minutes until golden brown.
6.   Serve warm with mustard on the side. The hot dogs can be cut in half for a cocktail party.

Vegetables

CUCUMBER BOATS WITH PRAWNS

Makes 24

1 straight cucumber	*1 dessertspoon tomato purée*
salt	*2 drops Tabasco sauce*
175 g (6 oz) full fat soft cheese	*24 peeled prawns*

PREPARATION TIME: 15 minutes, plus draining

1.   Score the length of the cucumber in straight lines, 5 mm (¼ inch) apart and cut into twenty-four 1 cm (½ inch) circles.
2.   Place the chunks in a colander, sprinkle with salt and leave to drain for 20 minutes.
3.   Put the cheese in a bowl and beat until soft. Add the tomato purée and Tabasco sauce.
4.   Place the mixture in a piping bag fitted with a star nozzle and pipe rosettes on each cucumber circle. Top each with a prawn and serve.

STUFFED RAW MUSHROOMS

Makes 40

40 button mushrooms
225 g (8 oz) full fat soft cheese

TO GARNISH:
25 g (1 oz) lumpfish roe
paprika pepper

PREPARATION TIME: 10 minutes

Select your own mushrooms at the greengrocers, making sure that they are as similar in size as possible and very fresh.

1. Remove the stalks from the mushrooms.
2. Beat the cheese to soften and place in a piping bag fitted with a large star nozzle. Pipe it into the mushroom caps.
3. Decorate half of the mushrooms with lumpfish roe and the rest with paprika pepper. Arrange on a serving dish.

🄰 The mushrooms can be prepared the day before, covered and kept in the refrigerator.

MUSHROOM BEIGNETS WITH CUCUMBER DIP

450 g (1 lb) button mushrooms
oil, for deep frying

CUCUMBER DIP:
300 ml (½ pint) mayonnaise
½ cucumber, peeled and
  finely chopped
½ onion, peeled and finely
  chopped
1 dessertspoon freshly
  chopped parsley

FRITTER BATTER:
150 g (5 oz) plain flour
pinch of salt
1 teaspoon dried yeast
175 ml (6 fl oz) warm water
1 tablespoon oil
1 egg white, whisked

TO GARNISH:
chopped parsley (optional)

PREPARATION TIME: 25-30 minutes, plus proving
COOKING TIME: 20-25 minutes
OVEN: 200°C, 400°F, Gas Mark 6

These mushrooms beignets are heated from frozen in a very hot oven. The cucumber dip can be made the day before.

1. To make the cucumber dip, mix together the mayonnaise, cucumber, onion and parsley. Chill for at least 1 hour.
2. Wipe the mushrooms with a clean, damp cloth and trim the stalks.
3. To make the batter, sift the flour and salt into a warm mixing bowl. Mix the yeast in half of the warm water and leave until frothy. Beat into the flour with the oil. Add the rest of the water and beat well.
4. Cover with a tea towel and leave in a warm place for 15-20 minutes. The mixture will rise slightly.

5.   Fold the egg white into the batter.
6.   Heat the oil to 180°-190°C/375°-350°F or until a cube of bread browns in 30 seconds.
7.   Using a slotted spoon, dip the mushrooms in the batter, a few at a time, then lower them into the oil. Fry for 3-4 minutes until golden brown. Drain the mushrooms on paper towels and cool on a wire tray.
8.   Pack the beignets in polythene bags, seal and freeze. F
9.   When required, place the frozen beignets on a baking sheet and bake in a preheated oven for 15-20 minutes.
10.   To serve, turn into a serving dish and spear with cock-tail sticks. Garnish with chopped parsley, if liked, and serve with the cucumber dip.

F The beignets can be frozen for up to 1 month.

Clockwise from the top: Stuffed celery boats; Stuffed raw mushrooms; Mushroom beignets with cucumber dip

STUFFED CELERY BOATS

Makes 25

1 head of celery, washed   *paprika pepper, for dusting*
175 g (6 oz) full fat soft cheese   *celery leaves, to garnish*

PREPARATION TIME: 15 minutes

These celery boats can be made the day before the party and refrigerated overnight.

1.   Cut the celery sticks into 2.5 cm (1 inch) lengths.
2.   Beat the cheese in a mixing bowl until smooth, then spoon or pipe into the celery pieces.
3.   Dust with paprika pepper before garnishing and serving.

TOMATOES STUFFED WITH CREAM CHEESE AND CHIVES

Makes 25

25 small firm cherry tomatoes
175 g (6 oz) full fat soft cheese
1 tablespoon chives, finely
   chopped

1 tablespoon single cream

TO GARNISH:
50 g (2 oz) lumpfish roe

PREPARATION TIME: 20 minutes

1. Cut a lid from the top of the tomatoes. Scoop out the seeds.
2. Mix the cheese, chives and cream together in a bowl. Place the mixture in a piping bag fitted with a 2½ cm (1 inch) plain nozzle and pipe into the tomato shells. Ⓐ
3. Serve garnished with lumpfish roe.

Ⓐ The tomatoes can be prepared 1 day in advance, if covered and chilled.

CHEESE BALLS WITH OLIVES

Makes 40

175 g (6 oz) Cheddar cheese,
   grated
100 g (4 oz) plain flour, sifted
100 g (4 oz) butter, melted
salt

½ teaspoon dry mustard
40 stuffed olives
finely chopped parsley, to
   garnish

PREPARATION TIME: 20 minutes
COOKING TIME: 10-15 minutes
OVEN: 200°C, 400°F, Gas Mark 6

The cheese balls can be frozen for up to 3 months and are cooked from frozen.

1.   Place the cheese, flour, butter, salt and mustard in a bowl and mix well together.
2.   Wrap 1 teaspoonful of the mixture around each olive.
3.   Place the balls on a baking sheet and open freeze. When frozen, wrap the balls carefully in a polythene bag, seal, label and return to the freezer.
4.   When required, place the frozen balls 5 cm (2 inches) apart on a baking sheet. Bake in a preheated oven for 10-15 minutes. Garnish and serve immediately.

DOLMAS

Makes 12 rolls

1 large green cabbage
100 g (4 oz) butter
1 medium carrot, diced
1 onion, chopped
1 small clove garlic, crushed
1 stick celery, chopped
50 g (2 oz) sunflower seeds
175 g (6 oz) walnuts, chopped
450 g (1 lb) ricotta cheese
225 g (8 oz) chopped apple
50 g (2 oz) raisins

4 tablespoons lemon juice
1-2 tablespoons soy sauce
1 tablespoon honey
salt
freshly ground black pepper
butter, for greasing

TO GARNISH:
150 ml (5 fl oz) yogurt or
    soured cream (optional)
leaves of celery

PREPARATION TIME: 1 hour
COOKING TIME: 25 minutes
OVEN: 160°C, 325°F, Gas Mark 3

1.   Boil the cabbage for 3-4 minutes. Be careful not to over-cook, or the leaves will break when rolled. Remove the first 12 leaves. (If there are not enough large leaves from 1 cabbage, parboil 2 and save the hearts to use for another dish.)
2.   Melt 75 g (3 oz) of the butter in a pan and sauté the carrot, onion, garlic, celery, sunflower seeds, and walnuts until the onion is transparent and the nuts roasted.
3.   Drain and combine the mixture with the cheese, apple, raisins, lemon juice, soy sauce and honey. Season to taste.
4.   Lay the cabbage leaves flat and cut out any thick stems. Place 2-3 tablespoons of filling near the base of each leaf. Roll tightly with the edges folded in. Place the cabbage parcels on a buttered baking sheet. Brush with butter, cover with foil and bake for 25 mintues until heated through.
5.   Serve on a bed or rice and garnish with celery leaves and yogurt or soured cream, if desired.

Fish

ROLLMOPS ON PUMPERNICKEL

Makes 32

25 g (1 oz) horseradish sauce
8 slices pumpernickel
1 × 240 g (8½ oz) jar
   rollmops, drained

TO GARNISH:
sprigs of parsley
radish roses (page 19)
radish slices

PREPARATION TIME: 15 minutes

---

1.   Spread a thin layer of horseradish sauce on each slice of pumpernickel.
2.   Cut each slice into 4 squares and arrange a small piece of rollmop on top.
3.   Serve garnished with parsley and radish.

DEEP FRIED SCAMPI WITH CAPER DIP

Serves 8

450 g (1 lb) unbreaded scampi
fritter batter (page 58)
fat, for deep frying

CAPER DIP:
300 ml (½ pint) mayonnaise

1 tablespoon capers
1 dessertspoon finely chopped
parsley

TO GARNISH:
paprika pepper

PREPARATION TIME: 25-30 minutes, plus proving
COOKING TIME: 5-10 minutes

This recipe for scampi with a tasty caper sauce makes an extremely appetizing dip for a party. The scampi may be served with cocktail sticks and a pretty bowl for the dip.

1.   To prepare the caper sauce, mix together the mayonnaise, capers and parsley.
2.   Wipe the scampi with a clean dry cloth.
3.   Toss the scampi in the batter until completely coated, then fry for 5-10 minutes. Drain on paper towels.
4.   Dust with paprika and serve with the caper dip. Garnish with lemon slices and a sprig of dill, if desired.

Rollmops on pumpernickel; Deep fried scampi with caper dip

GOUJONS OF SOLE

Serves 12

1 × 1.25 kg (2½ lb) sole,
 filleted
plain flour, for coating
1-2 eggs, beaten

fresh breadcrumbs, for
 coating
oil, for deep frying

PREPARATION TIME: 25 minutes, plus chilling
COOKING TIME: 20 minutes
OVEN: 120°C, 250°F, Gas Mark ½

These goujons are delicious served either on their own, on a
cocktail stick or with a dip, such as sauce tartare, or with
wedges of lemon.

1. Skin the sole and wash and drain well in a colander.
2. Cut the fish into strips 1 cm (½ inch) wide and 4 cm (1½
inches) long (approximately 24-32 strips).
3. Coat the strips in flour, then dip into egg and roll in
breadcrumbs. Chill for 30 minutes.
4. Heat the oil to 180°-190°C/350°-375°F or until a cube of
bread browns in 30 seconds. Lower the goujons into the oil 8
at a time and cook until browned.
5. Drain on paper towels and keep warm in a low oven
while cooking the remainder. Serve immediately, garnished with lemon wedges and parsley sprigs, if desired.

COURGETTES STUFFED WITH TARAMASALATA

Makes 24

14 small courgettes, washed
175 g (6 oz) taramasalata
 (page 49)

TO GARNISH:
paprika pepper

PREPARATION TIME: 20 minutes

Courgettes can be prepared and filled the day before the
party and refrigerated.

1. Cut the courgettes in half lengthways. Scoop out the
centre with a tiny melon baller or a teaspoon, then cut across
in 4 cm (1½ inch) pieces.
2. Place the taramasalata in a piping bag fitted with a
2½ cm (1 inch) star nozzle and pipe into the courgette
halves. Sprinkle with a little paprika before serving.

Clockwise from the top: Courgettes stuffed with taramasalata;
Stuffed eggs with prawns; Goujons of sole

STUFFED EGGS WITH PRAWNS

Makes 24

12 hard-boiled eggs
25 g (1 oz) butter, softened
2 tablespoons mayonnaise
1 teaspoon curry powder
salt

freshly ground black pepper

TO GARNISH:
shredded lettuce (optional)
50 g (2 oz) peeled prawns

PREPARATION TIME: 15-20 minutes

---

1. Halve the eggs lengthways, scoop out the yolks and place them in a basin.
2. Mix together the yolks, butter, mayonnaise, curry powder and salt and pepper. Add more mayonnaise if the mixture is too stiff.
3. Place the mixture in a piping bag fitted with a star nozzle and pipe back into the eggs. Ⓐ
4. Serve on a bed of shredded lettuce, if desired, and garnish with the prawns.

Ⓐ The stuffed eggs can be prepared the day before, covered and refrigerated.

SMOKED SALMON AND CRAB ROLLS

Makes 24

1 × 225 g (8 oz) can white crab
    meat
50 g (2 oz) full fat soft cheese
25 g (1 oz) capers, chopped
2 tablespoons mayonnaise
salt
freshly ground black pepper
few drops of Tabasco
1 teaspoon gelatine
2 teaspoons Cognac, warmed

225 g (8 oz) smoked salmon,
    cut into 24 strips, 5 cm
    (2 inches) wide
6 slices brown bread, buttered
    and cut into 24 × 5 cm (2
    inch) rounds

TO GARNISH:
1 lemon, cut into wedges
sprigs of dill

PREPARATION TIME: 20 minutes, plus chilling

These rolls should be chilled in a refrigerator for a few hours before serving or they can be made the day before.

1.　In a bowl, mix together the crab meat, cheese, capers, mayonnaise, salt, pepper and Tabasco.
2.　Dissolve the gelatine in the Cognac in a bowl over a pan of hot water. Add to the crab mixture. Allow to cool and set.
3.　Put 1 teaspoon of the crab mixture on each slice of smoked salmon and roll up. Cover and chill for at least 2 hours, or overnight.
4.　Place the rolls on small rounds of buttered brown bread and serve garnished with lemon wedges and dill.

SALMON WITH CUCUMBER AND YOGURT SALAD

Serves 24

1 × 3½ kg (8 lb) salmon,
  gutted and cleaned, with
  the head left on

COURT BOUILLON:
1 carrot, sliced
1 onion, sliced
6 peppercorns
1 teaspoon salt
150 ml (¼ pint) white wine

TO GARNISH:
2 lemons, sliced
½ cucumber, sliced thinly

1 bunch radishes, sliced thinly
6 unpeeled prawns
fennel or dill
olive slice

CUCUMBER AND YOGURT
  SALAD:
3 cucumbers, skinned and
  sliced
1 litre (1¾ pints) plain
  unsweetened yogurt
1 tablespoon chopped chives

PREPARATION TIME: 20 minutes
COOKING TIME: 1 hour, plus cooling

Salmon has such a delicately textured flesh that it must be cooked with care. Do not let the liquid boil. Salmon can be cooked the day before it is to be eaten and kept, covered, in the refrigerator.

1. Lay the fish on the drainer of a fish kettle and just cover with cold water. Add the court bouillon ingredients.
2. Place the fish kettle on the hob, cover and bring slowly to the boil, allowing about 40 minutes, then immediately turn the heat off and allow the salmon to cool in the water (about 6-8 hours).
3. Lift out the fish, drain well, then skin.
4. Lay the fish on a platter and garnish: arrange fennel or dill around the edge with the prawns and slices of lemon. Cover the salmon with overlapping slices of cucumber and radish, to resemble scales. Put the olive slice in the eye socket.
5. To make the salad, combine the cucumber slices with the yogurt and sprinkle with chopped chives.

When choosing a salmon, make sure that the flesh is bright red in colour and the scales very shiny. A good salmon should have a small head, thick shoulders and a small tail. The months of March through August are the best times to buy fresh salmon, although in June and July the fish is more expensive due to high demand. Leftover small pieces of salmon may be used in sandwiches, made into a pie with a good béchamel sauce, or transformed into a mousse or pâté.

Left: Salmon with cucumber and yogurt salad; *Right:* Smoked salmon and crab rolls

Meat

YORK HAM WITH PEACHES

Serves 20

1 × 4.5 kg (10 lb) leg joint of
  gammon, soaked overnight
  in cold water
4 bay leaves
20 peppercorns
1 onion, sliced
75 g (3 oz) demerara sugar
15 whole cloves

2 × 425 g (15 oz) can peach
  halves, drained and juice
  reserved
1 × 275 ml (9 fl oz) bottle of
  medium dry cider

TO GARNISH:
sprigs of parsley

PREPARATION TIME: 15 minutes, plus chilling overnight
COOKING TIME: 3 hours 55 minutes
OVEN: 200°C, 400°F, Gas Mark 6

York hams are very sweet and delicate in flavour. Placed on a
ham stand, they make a very good centerpiece for a buffet
table. If you don't have a ham stand, ask your butcher to lend
you one; it makes carving at the table a lot easier. Carve a few
slices before the party for quicker serving.

1.   Place the soaked ham in a large saucepan of cold water
with the bay leaves, peppercorns and onion. Bring to the
boil, skim the surface, and then simmer until cooked, about
3½ hours. Allow to cool in the cooking liquid.
2.   Lift out the ham, remove the skin and place in a roasting
tin.
3.   Pour the peach juice and cider over the ham. Cover the
ham with sugar and stick the cloves into the fat. Bake in a
preheated oven for 25 minutes, basting after 10 minutes,
until golden brown.
4.   Allow to go completely cold and refrigerate overnight.
5.   Serve garnished with peach halves and parsley sprigs.

Top: York ham with peaches; *Bottom:* Hawaiian chicken

HAWAIIAN CHICKEN

Serves 8

1 × 1.75 kg (4 lb) chicken,
  cooked
450 ml (¾ pint) mayonnaise
3 tablespoons double or
  whipping cream, whipped
2 tablespoons sherry or white
  wine
225 g (8 oz) white grapes,
  seedless, or skinned, halved
  and seeded
3 sticks of celery, washed,

trimmed and diced
1 × 225 g (8 oz) can of
  pineapple rings, drained
  and diced
75 g (3 oz) walnuts, roughly
  chopped

TO GARNISH:
2 tablespoons finely chopped
  parsley

PREPARATION TIME: 25 minutes

This dish has a delicate flavour and is delicious served with a rice salad. Remember that you will only get 1.25 kg (2½ lbs) of cooked meat from a 1.75 kg (4 lb) chicken.

1. Joint the chicken with care and remove the skin and bones. Cut into bite-sized pieces. F
2. Put the mayonnaise in a large mixing bowl and add the cream and sherry or white wine.
3. Carefully fold in the chicken pieces, grapes, celery, pineapple and walnuts. A
4. Arrange on a large oval serving dish. Sprinkle the chopped parsley diagonally over the top.

A This dish can be prepared the day before, covered and refrigerated overnight.
F The chicken can be frozen for up to 2 months.

Top: Chicken drumsticks; *Bottom:* Roast turkey with lemon stuffing balls

ROAST TURKEY WITH LEMON STUFFING BALLS

Serves 15-20

1 × 6.5 kg (14 lb) turkey
1 onion, peeled and halved
100 g (4 oz) butter, softened
salt
freshly ground black pepper

LEMON STUFFING BALLS:
225 g (8 oz) minced veal
175 g (6 oz) fresh white
  breadcrumbs
grated rind of 1 lemon

2 tablespoons lemon juice
1 tablespoon finely chopped
  parsley
175 g (6 oz) butter, melted
2 eggs, beaten
salt
freshly ground black pepper

TO GARNISH:
watercress

PREPARATION TIME: 35 minutes, plus chilling overnight
COOKING TIME: 5-5¼ hours
OVEN: 160°C, 325°F, Gas Mark 3
then 180°C, 350°F, Gas Mark 4

When serving a turkey cold it is better to make individual stuffing balls, cooked separately for easy serving. Place an onion or lemon for flavour in the cavity of the bird during cooking. If using a frozen turkey read the defrosting instructions carefully. Prepare and cook the turkey the day before the party.

---

1. Place the onion halves in the cavity of the bird and rub the skin lavishly all over with butter. Season with salt and pepper.
2. Place the turkey in a roasting pan and cover with buttered foil. Bake in a preheated oven at the lower temperature for 4½-4¾ hours, removing the foil 45 minutes before the end of cooking time to allow the skin to brown.
3. To test if the bird is done, pierce the thickest part of the thigh with a skewer. If the juices run clear, the bird is cooked.
4. Remove the turkey from the oven and transfer to a wire tray. Leave to go completely cold and, if possible, refrigerate overnight.
5. To make the stuffing balls, mix together the veal, breadcrumbs, lemon rind, lemon juice, parsley, butter, eggs and salt and pepper.
6. Shape the mixture into 20 small balls and place in a greased ovenproof dish. Cover with foil and bake in the oven preheated at the higher temperature for 30 minutes. Leave to go cold, then chill for at least 2 hours. ⅎ
7. Serve the turkey in slices on a large serving dish with the stuffing balls and watercress.

ⅎ The stuffing balls can be frozen for up to 1 month. Thaw for 2 hours at room temperature.

CHICKEN DRUMSTICKS

Serves 40

8 tablespoons lemon juice
275 g (10 oz) butter, melted
3 cloves garlic, crushed
2 teaspoons dried rosemary

salt
freshly ground black pepper
40 chicken drumsticks

PREPARATION TIME: 40 minutes, plus chilling
COOKING TIME: 25-30 minutes
OVEN: 200°C, 400°F, Gas Mark 6

Drumsticks are always very popular at parties and look good served in a basket. Make sure that you have lots of paper napkins available for greasy fingers. For an alternative coating, see the recipe for Barbecue dip, page 72.

1. In a bowl mix together the lemon juice, butter, garlic, rosemary, salt and pepper.
2. Brush each drumstick thoroughly with the mixture.
3. Place the drumsticks in roasting tins and cook, uncovered, in a preheated oven for 25-30 minutes. Turn once during cooking. The skin should be crisp.
4. Lift the drumsticks out on to a wire tray to cool. Chill in the refrigerator for at least 2 hours.
5. Place cutlet frills over the ends of the drumsticks and serve.

SAVOURY MEAT BALLS WITH BARBECUE DIP

Makes 24

450 g (1 lb) sausage meat
1 garlic clove, crushed
4 tablespoons apple purée
1 dessertspoon finely chopped
    parsley
1 teaspoon dried thyme
salt
freshly ground black pepper
1 egg, beaten
1 dessertspoon plain flour
oil, for shallow frying

BARBECUE DIP:
1 garlic clove, crushed
¼ teaspoon salt
1 teaspoon dry mustard

1 teaspoon sugar
1 teaspoon paprika pepper
½ teaspoon freshly ground
    black pepper
600 ml (1 pint) tomato juice
3 tablespoons vinegar
1 tablespoon tomato ketchup
1 tablespoon Worcestershire
    sauce
2 tablespoons horseradish
    sauce
1 small onion, finely chopped
50 g (2 oz) hard margarine

TO GARNISH:
sprigs of parsley (optional)

PREPARATION TIME: 30 minutes
COOKING TIME: 40-45 minutes

Guests really appreciate hot food served on a cold day. The meat balls and dip freeze well for up to 2 months and take 2 hours to thaw. Freeze the meat balls before cooking. The dip is good with all savoury dishes.

1. Place the sausage meat in a bowl and add the garlic, apple purée, parsley, thyme and salt and pepper to taste.
2. Bind the mixture with the beaten egg.
3. With floured hands, roll the mixture into balls the size of a walnut.
4. Heat the oil in a frying pan. Fry the meatballs, a few at a time, for 10-15 minutes until golden brown. Drain on paper towels and keep warm.

5. To make the barbecue dip, place all the ingredients in a saucepan and bring to the boil. Simmer until reduced by half, about 30 minutes.
6. Spear the meat balls with cocktail sticks and serve garnished with parsley sprigs, if desired. Serve the dip separately.

CONTREFILET OF BEEF

Serves 20

3.5 kg (8 lb) contrefilet or fillet of beef
25-50 g (1-2 oz) dripping
salt
freshly ground black pepper

TO GARNISH:
watercress
tomatoes, quartered

PREPARATION TIME: 10 minutes, plus chilling overnight
COOKING TIME: 1 hour 15 minutes
OVEN: 200°C, 400°F, Gas Mark 6

1. Cover the joint with dripping and season.
2. Place in a roasting pan and roast in a preheated oven for 1 hour 15 minutes, basting at regular intervals.
3. When cooked, transfer to a dish and allow the meat to become completely cold. Cover with cling film and refrigerate overnight.
4. Carve the joint into thin slices and arrange on a serving dish. Garnish with watercress and tomatoes and serve with mustard and/or horseradish sauce.

MELON BALLS WITH PARMA HAM

Serves 20-30

1 honeydew melon, halved and seeded

100 g (4 oz) Parma ham, cut into thin strips

PREPARATION TIME: 20 minutes, plus chilling

1. Scoop out the flesh from one half of the melon with a melon baller. Place the balls in a bowl.
2. Cut the second half of melon into small cubes or sticks 2½ cm (1 inch) × 1 cm (½ inch) and wrap the strips of Parma ham around them. Cover and chill the cubes and balls in the refrigerator for 2 hours.
3. Arrange the melon and ham chunks on a serving dish, pile the melon balls in the centre and serve.

Clockwise from the top: Contrefilet of beef; Melon balls with parma ham; Savoury meat balls with barbecue dip

HAM CORNETS WITH LIVER PÂTÉ FILLING

Serves 6

12 square slices ham shoulder
12 metal cornet moulds

LIVER PÂTÉ FILLING:
175 g (6 oz) butter, softened
1 large onion, finely chopped
1 clove garlic
350 g (12 oz) chicken livers

1 small bouquet garni
salt
freshly ground black pepper
1 tablespoon brandy

TO GARNISH:
3 stuffed olives, sliced
1 bunch watercress

PREPARATION TIME: 30 minutes, plus chilling
COOKING TIME: 15 minutes

You can use any of your favourite smooth pâté or mousse recipes to fill these cornets.

1.   To make the pâté, melt 25 g (1 oz) of the butter in a pan and soften the onion and garlic until just beginning to colour.
2.   Add the liver, bouquet garni, salt and pepper and fry together for about 3 minutes. Leave to cool, then remove the bouquet garni.
3.   Chop the mixture very finely and pass through a fine sieve, or liquidize. Beat in the remaining butter and add the brandy. Set aside.
4.   Roll the slices of ham into a cornet shape and carefully slide into the cornet moulds. Trim the ham about 5 mm (¼ inch) above the mould with scissors. Chop the ham trimmings finely and add to the pâté.
5.   Fill the ham cornets with the pâté, and garnish each with 2 slices of stuffed olives.
6.   Leave in a cool place to firm for 2-3 hours. 🄰
7.   Remove the cornets from their moulds.
8.   Serve on a bed of watercress, if desired.

🄰 The cornets can be prepared 1 day in advance and refrigerated.

PRESSED TONGUE

Serves 15

1 × 1.75 kg (4 lb) ox tongue,
    rolled up into a round shape
    and tied firmly with string
2 large onions, chopped
2 carrots, chopped
2 celery stalks, chopped
8 peppercorns

1 × 25 g (1 oz) packet aspic
    jelly

TO GARNISH:
watercress
cucumber slices, halved
stuffed olives, sliced

PREPARATION TIME: 35 minutes, plus cooling and chilling overnight
COOKING TIME: 4-5 hours

If you have a good butcher he will almost certainly prepare and salt the tongue ready for cooking.

1.   Rinse the tongue in cold water and place in a large pan with enough cold water to cover the tongue.
2.   Add the onions, carrots, celery and peppercorns.
3.   Bring slowly to the boil, skimming if necessary. Cover the pan and simmer gently for 4-5 hours, until tender.
4.   Allow the tongue to cool slightly in the liquor for about 1 hour, before lifting out and draining.
5.   Remove the string, and any bones and skin, from the tongue.
6.   Shape the tongue into a tight curl and fit into a circular 23 cm (9 inch) cake tin. Cover with a plate which fits inside the tin and place a heavy weight, about 3 kg (7 lb), on the plate. Leave until cold.
7.   Make up 300 ml (½ pint) aspic jelly according to the packet instructions and, when it is cool, pour into the tin. Replace the plate and weight and refrigerate overnight. F
8.   Turn out on to a serving plate and garnish.

F The tongue can be frozen for up to 2 months. Thaw for 4-5 hours at room temperature, or overnight in the refrigerator.

Top: Pressed tongue: *Bottom:* Ham cornets with liver pâté filling

SALAMI CORNETS

Makes 32

16 slices German salami, rind   *175 g (6 oz) full fat soft cheese*
removed

PREPARATION TIME: 20-25 minutes, plus chilling

German salami is used for the cornets as it holds its shape when stuck together.

1.   Cut each salami slice in half and shape into a cornet, pressing firmly together.
2.   Place the soft cheese in a piping bag fitted with a 2½ cm (1 inch) star nozzle and pipe rosettes into each cornet. F
3.   Chill the cornets for 1 hour before serving.

F The cornets can be frozen for up to 1 month. Thaw for at least 1 hour at room temperature.

MINI KEBABS

Makes 24

24 × 1.25 cm (½ inch) cubes
    cooked ham
3 green peppers, cored, seeded
    and cut into 2.5 cm (1 inch)
    squares)
3 red peppers, cored, seeded
    and cut into 2.5 cm (1 inch)
    squares
6 rashers streaky bacon, rolled
    up, grilled until crisp and

    cut into 4 slices
12 cocktail sausages, cooked
    and cut in half
24 × 1.25 cm (½ inch) cubes
    Cheddar cheese
24 pickled silverskin onions

TO GARNISH:
1 lettuce (optional)

PREPARATION TIME: 20 minutes
COOKING TIME: 10 minutes

1.   Arrange a selection of the above ingredients on cocktail sticks. A
2.   Serve cold, or brush with melted butter and grill gently for 10 minutes, turning once.
3.   To serve, arrange the mini kebabs on a bed of lettuce, if desired.

A The mini kebabs can be prepared the day before and refrigerated.

COCKTAIL SAUSAGES WITH MUSTARD DIP

Serves 30

1.5 kg (3 lb) cocktail sausages
2 dessertspoons made mustard

TO GARNISH:
sprigs of parsley (optional)

PREPARATION TIME: 10-15 minutes
COOKING TIME: 25 minutes
OVEN: 200°C, 400°F, Gas Mark 6

Sausages are a must at any party as they suit all ages and tastes. Serve them warm on cocktail sticks.

1.   Separate the sausages and place on a baking sheet. Cook in a hot oven for 25 minutes until well browned, turning once during cooking. Drain the sausages on paper towels.
2.   Spear the sausages with cocktail sticks and serve warm in an ovenproof dish with a small pot of mustard in the centre. Garnish with parsley sprigs, if desired.

Clockwise from the top: Cocktail sausages with mustard dip; Salami cornets; Mini kebabs

DEVILS ON HORSEBACK

Makes 25-30

450 g (1 lb) streaky bacon rashers	*2 × 400 g (14 oz) cans prunes, stoned*

PREPARATION TIME: 20-25 minutes
COOKING TIME: 20 minutes
OVEN: 230°C, 450°F, Gas Mark 8

1. Halve the bacon slices and roll each piece around a prune.
2. Thread the rolls on cocktail sticks and place on baking sheets. Bake in a preheated oven for 20 minutes, until the bacon is brown and crisp, turning once during cooking.
3. Drain on paper towels and remove the skewers.

MINIATURE CORNISH PASTIES

Makes 12

FILLING:
225 g (8 oz) potatoes, peeled and diced
1 tablespoon oil
225 g (8 oz) minced meat
75 g (3 oz) onion, finely chopped
1 dessertspoon tomato purée
1 teaspoon Worcestershire sauce
few drops of Tabasco sauce
1 beef stock cube dissolved in

1 tablespoon hot water
salt
freshly ground black pepper

PASTRY:
225 g (8 oz) plain flour
1 teaspoon salt
75 g (3 oz) lard
50 g (2 oz) margarine
3 tablespoons water
1 egg or milk, to glaze (optional)

PREPARATION TIME: 1 hour, plus cooling
COOKING TIME: 30 minutes
OVEN: 200°C, 400°F, Gas Mark 6

1. To make the filling, boil the potatoes in salted water for about 10 minutes. Drain and cool. Heat the oil in a frying pan and fry the mince and onion until brown. Add the tomato purée, Worcestershire and Tabasco sauces, beef stock, salt, pepper and potatoes and leave to cool for 1 hour.
2. To make the pastry, sieve the flour and salt into a bowl and rub in the fats until the mixture resembles fine bread-crumbs. Add sufficient water to make a dough.
3. Roll out thinly and cut into 10 cm (4 inch) rounds.
4. Dampen the edge of one half of each round. Place a heaped teaspoon of filling in the centre and flute the edges together. Place the pasties on a baking sheet and bake in a preheated oven for 30 minutes. Serve hot.

Clockwise from the top: Miniature Cornish pasties; Cocktail Scotch eggs; Devils on horseback

COCKTAIL SCOTCH EGGS

Makes 12

450 g (1 lb) sausage meat
1 teaspoon mixed herbs
2 teaspoons Worcestershire
sauce
plain flour

12 hard-boiled eggs (size 6)
2 eggs, beaten
225 g (8 oz) dried breadcrumbs
fat or oil, for deep frying
cress, to garnish

PREPARATION TIME: 20-25 minutes
COOKING TIME: 5-10 minutes

---

1. Mix the sausage meat, mixed herbs and Worcestershire sauce together. Divide the mixture into 12 portions.
2. Press the portions into neat squares on a floured board.
3. Wrap the squares round the eggs and coat first in beaten egg, then in breadcrumbs.
4. Heat the fat or oil to 180-190°C/350-375°F, or until a cube of bread browns in 30 seconds.
5. Fry the Scotch eggs, 4 at a time, for approximately 5 minutes. Drain thoroughly on paper towels. A
6. When cold, cut the eggs in halves or quarters and serve.

A The Scotch eggs can be made up to 2 days in advance of the party and refrigerated.

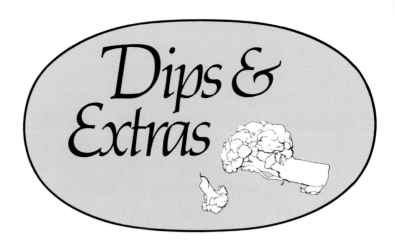

Dips & Extras

ARTICHOKE DIP

Serves 8

2 cloves garlic, crushed
400 ml (14 fl oz) mayonnaise
½ teaspoon cayenne pepper
freshly ground black pepper
4 tablespoons Parmesan
  cheese, grated

2 × 400 g (14 oz) can artichoke
  hearts, chopped
paprika, to taste

TO SERVE:
crudités (page 82) or warm
  crusty French bread

PREPARATION TIME: 10 minutes
COOKING TIME: 20 minutes
OVEN: 180°C, 350°F, Gas Mark 4

1.   Place the garlic, mayonnaise, cayenne pepper, black pepper and Parmesan cheese in a bowl and mix together thoroughly. Gently fold in the chopped artichokes and paprika pepper.
2.   Pour the mixture into an ovenproof dish and bake in a preheated oven for 20 minutes, or until bubbling.
3.   Serve immediately with crusty French bread or as a dip with crudités.

HERBY CHICKEN WITH CUCUMBER DIP

Serves 10

4 × 175 g (6 oz) chicken
  breasts
50 g (2 oz) seasoned plain flour
1 beaten egg
75 g (3 oz) dry herby stuffing
  mix

1 tablespoon oil
50 g (2 oz) butter
½ cucumber, chopped
1 Spanish onion, chopped
150 ml (¼ pint) mayonnaise

PREPARATION TIME: 20 minutes, plus chilling

1. Cut each chicken breast into 6 strips and coat with seasoned flour, then in the egg, and stuffing mix.
2. Melt the oil and butter in a pan and fry the chicken strips for about 5 minutes. Allow to cool, then chill for 1 hour.
3. Mix the vegetable ingredients together with the mayonnaise and chill the dip for 2 hours before serving with the chicken pieces.

AVOCADO DIP

Serves 8

1 small onion, finely chopped
1 green pepper, finely
   chopped
2 large, soft avocados, skinned
   and mashed with a potato
   masher
350 g (12 oz) full fat soft
   cheese
3 tablespoons lemon juice

salt
freshly ground black pepper
1 tablespoon chopped parsley
2 tablespoons snipped chives
100 g (4 oz) soured cream

TO SERVE:
crudités (page 82) or warm
   crusty French bread

PREPARATION TIME: 15-20 minutes, plus chilling

---

1. Blend all the ingredients together well.
2. Spoon the mixture into a serving dish, cover and chill well in the refrigerator for at least 2 hours before serving.

From the top: Herby chicken with cucumber dip; Artichoke dip; Avocado dip

From the top: Fresh mushroom mélange; Potted cheese with crudités; Stuffed dates

POTTED CHEESE WITH CRUDITÉS

Serves 8-10

POTTED CHEESE:
100 g (4 oz) butter or margarine
225 g (8 oz) mixed cheeses, including a little blue cheese, grated or crumbled
pinch of salt
freshly ground black pepper
¼ teaspoon dry mustard
2-3 tablespoons port or sherry
3-4 tablespoons single cream

CRUDITÉS:
4 celery sticks, cut into matchsticks

1 green or yellow pepper, de-seeded and cut into matchsticks
1 red pepper, de-seeded and cut into matchsticks or 12 baby carrots
½ cucumber, cut into matchsticks
2 medium carrots, cut into matchsticks
½ small cauliflower, broken into small florets

TO GARNISH:
1 tablespoon chopped parsley

PREPARATION TIME: 45 minutes

1. To make the potted cheese, cream the butter in a bowl until soft.
2. Work the cheeses into the butter and add the salt, pepper and mustard.
3. Add sufficient wine and cream to make a soft pâté.
4. Put the potted cheese in a small serving bowl, garnish with parsley and stand in the centre of a large serving plate.
5. Arrange the prepared crudités attractively on the plate around the potted cheese.

FRESH MUSHROOM MÉLANGE

Serves 8

175 g (6 oz) full fat soft cheese
4 tablespoons mayonnaise
½ teaspoon paprika pepper
½ teaspoon Tabasco sauce
450 g (1 lb) button
    mushrooms, finely chopped
1 large onion, peeled and
chopped
2 teaspoons lemon juice
2 tablespoons finely chopped
    parsley
freshly ground black pepper.
sprigs of parsley, to garnish

PREPARATION TIME: 10 minutes, plus chilling

1. Place the cheese, mayonnaise, paprika and Tabasco in a bowl and mix well together.
2. Gently fold in the mushrooms, onion, lemon juice and parsley. Add black pepper to taste.
3. Turn into a serving dish and refrigerate for 15 minutes. Garnish and serve with crudités or spread on croûtons.

STUFFED DATES

Makes 24-30

225 g (8 oz) full fat soft cheese
grated rind of 1 orange
1 × 225 g (8 oz) box of dried
    dates, stones removed
    or 30 fresh dates

PREPARATION TIME: 15 minutes

These can be made the day before the party and kept, covered, in the refrigerator.

1. In a mixing bowl, beat the cheese until smooth. Stir in the orange rind.
2. Pipe the cheese mixture into the dates.

CHEESE SHELLS

Makes 14-16

2 egg whites, whisked
50 g (2 oz) Parmesan cheese,
    finely grated
salt
freshly ground black pepper

pinch of cayenne pepper
oil, for deep frying

TO GARNISH:
Parmesan cheese, grated
cayenne pepper, for dusting

PREPARATION TIME: 15 minutes
COOKING TIME: 10 minutes

These cheese meringues are very popular served as a savoury at a cocktail party.

1. In a mixing bowl whisk the egg whites until stiff.
2. Gently fold the cheese, salt, pepper and cayenne into the egg whites.
3. Heat the oil to 180°-190°C/350°-375°F or until a cube of bread browns in 30 seconds. Lower dessertspoons of the mixture into the oil, 8 at a time, and cook until golden brown.
4. Drain on paper towels, then sprinkle with Parmesan cheese and cayenne pepper. Serve immediately.

EGG AND BACON ROLLS

Makes 36

12 slices white bread, crusts
    removed
100 g (4 oz) margarine, melted
6 eggs, scrambled (see page
    52)

3 rashers streaky bacon, finely
    chopped and fried
salt
freshly ground black pepper

PREPARATION TIME: 20 minutes
COOKING TIME: 20-30 minutes
OVEN: 180°C, 350°F, Gas Mark 4

1. Using a rolling pin, roll the slices of bread until thin.
2. Brush one side of a slice of bread with a little melted margarine and spread on some of the egg and bacon. Roll up like a Swiss roll and secure either end with a cocktail stick, then cut in half. Repeat for all 18 slices. 🅰
3. Place the rolls on a greased baking sheet, brush with the remaining margarine and bake in a preheated oven for 20-30 minutes, until crisp and golden brown.
4. Cut the rolls in half and serve immediately.

🅰 The egg and bacon rolls can be prepared the day before, then cooked just before serving.

From the top: Cheese shells; Almond cheeses; Egg and bacon rolls

ALMOND AND PINEAPPLE CHEESES

Makes 12

350 g (12 oz) full fat soft
  cheese
1 × 225 g (8 oz) can crushed

pineapple, drained
100 g (4 oz) crushed almonds,
  toasted

PREPARATION TIME: 15 minutes, plus chilling

The cheeses do not freeze well as the pineapple makes them too moist. They can be prepared 2 days in advance, if covered and chilled.

1.   Place the cheese and pineapple in a bowl and mix together thoroughly.
2.   Form the mixture into 12 small balls the size of an olive.
3.   Roll in the almonds to coat evenly and chill in the refrigerator for 1 hour.

Desserts

HAZELNUT TORTE

Makes one 20 cm (8 inch) torte to serve 8

MERINGUE:
4 egg whites
225 g (8 oz) caster sugar
200 g (7 oz) hazelnuts, skinned and crushed
few drops of vanilla essence

TO DECORATE:
300 ml (½ pint) double or whipping cream, whipped
100 g (4 oz) fresh or frozen raspberries, thawed
8 whole hazelnuts
sifted icing sugar, to dust

PREPARATION TIME: 20 minutes
COOKING TIME: 40 minutes
OVEN: 190°C, 375°F, Gas Mark 5

This torte should be eaten on the same day as assembled. The base can be made in advance and frozen.

1. Draw a 20 cm (8 inch) circle on a piece of greaseproof paper. Place on a baking sheet.
2. Whisk the egg whites until stiff, then whisk in the sugar, a tablespoon at a time. Continue whisking until the meringue is very stiff and holds its shape. Carefully fold in 175 g (6 oz) of the hazelnuts and the vanilla essence.
3. Spoon the mixture on to the prepared circle and bake in a preheated oven for 40 minutes. Leave to cool. Remove the lining paper and place on a wire tray. Ⓕ
4. Spread two-thirds of the cream on to the meringue case. Using the remaining cream, pipe 16 rosettes on top of the cream. Top every other rosette with a whole hazelnut. Fill the centre with raspberries and sprinkle with the remaining hazelnuts. If fresh fruit is used, dust with icing sugar.

Ⓕ The base can be frozen for up to 2 months. Thaw for 2 hours at room temperature.

Top: Hazelnut torte; *Bottom:* Chocolate cases with ginger

CHOCOLATE CASES WITH GINGER SYLLABUB

Makes 12

350 g (12 oz) plain chocolate
24 paper cake cases
375 ml (15 fl oz) double or
* whipping cream, whipped*
100 ml (4 fl oz) brandy
2 dessertspoons stem ginger,

* finely chopped*
1 tablespoon syrup from stem
* ginger*

TO DECORATE:
chocolate curls

PREPARATION TIME: 45 minutes, plus chilling

Use the paper cases in pairs to give 12 of double thickness. Any flavour ice cream or syllabub can be used in place of the ginger syllabub.

1.   Melt the chocolate in a dish in a cool oven. Using the back of a dessertspoon, coat the inside of the paper cases with a thick layer of chocolate. Leave until cold, then peel off the paper cases.
2.   Whip the cream, brandy and syrup together until the mixture just holds its shape. Fold in the chopped ginger. Chill well.
3.   Spoon the syllabub into the chocolate cups and decorate with chocolate curls. ꘙ

ꘙ These can be frozen for up to 2 months. Thaw for 1 hour at room temperature.

VIENNESE CURD CAKE WITH APRICOT SAUCE

Makes one 20 cm (8 inch) cake to serve 8

40 g (1½ oz) butter
175 g (6 oz) digestive biscuits,
* crushed*
120 g (4½ oz) caster sugar
350 g (12 oz) curd cheese
2-3 drops vanilla essence
15 g (½ oz) gelatine soaked in
* 5 tablespoons water*
300 ml (½ pint) double or
* whipping cream, whipped*

3 egg whites, whisked
toasted flaked almonds, to
* decorate*

APRICOT SAUCE (optional):
1 × 425 g (15 oz) can of
* apricots*
grated rind of 1 lemon
2 tablespoons lemon juice

PREPARATION TIME: 30 minutes, plus chilling

This cake and sauce will freeze beautifully.

1. Melt the butter in a pan. Mix in the biscuit crumbs and 25 g (1 oz) of the caster sugar.
2. Spread the mixture over the base of a 20 cm (8 inch) loose-bottomed cake tin.
3. Cream the cheese with the rest of the sugar and vanilla essence.
4. Stir the soaked gelatine in a bowl over a pan of hot water until dissolved, then stir into the cheese mixture.
5. Mix the whisked egg whites with two-thirds of the whipped cream and fold into the cheese mixture. Spoon over the biscuit base and chill for 2-4 hours or overnight.
6. Remove the cake from the tin. Ⓕ Decorate with the remaining cream and sprinkle with flaked almonds.
7. Add the lemon rind and juice to the apricots and their juice. Liquidize the ingredients together. Ⓕ Pour the sauce into a serving jug and serve with portions of the cake.

Ⓕ The cake and sauce can be frozen for up to 1 month. Thaw for 2 hours at room temperature.

CHOCOLATE PROFITEROLES

Serves 12

CHOUX PASTRY:
100 g (4 oz) margarine
300 ml (½ pint) water
150 g (5 oz) plain flour, sifted
4 small eggs, beaten

CHOCOLATE SAUCE:
175 g (6 oz) plain chocolate

300 ml (½ pint) water
100 g (4 oz) sugar
about 4 teaspoons cornflour
* (optional)*

FILLING:
450 ml (¾ pint) double or
* whipping cream, whipped*

PREPARATION TIME: 30 minutes
COOKING TIME: 40-45 minutes
OVEN: 220°C, 425°F, Gas Mark 7
then 190°C, 375°F, Gas Mark 5

1.   Melt the margarine in a large pan, add the water and bring to the boil.
2.   Add the flour all at once, and beat until the mixture leaves the side of the pan. Cool slightly.
3.   Add the eggs a little at a time, beating vigorously. Be careful not to get the mixture too wet – it should be smooth, shiny and should hold its shape. If too soft, it will not rise.
4.   Place the mixture in a piping bag fitted with a plain 1 cm (½ inch) nozzle and pipe small mounds on a dampened greased baking sheet.
5.   Bake in a preheated oven for 10 minutes, then lower the heat and cook for a further 20-25 minutes until dark golden brown.
6.   When cooked, make a slit in the side of each bun with a sharp knife. This will prevent them from going soggy. Cool on a wire tray. F
7.   To make the chocolate sauce, melt the chocolate with the water in a saucepan over a gentle heat.
8.   When smooth, add the sugar and bring to the boil. Simmer for 15 minutes until syrupy.
9.   If the chocolate is too thin, add the cornflour mixed to a paste with a little water. Bring back to the boil and cook for 2 minutes. Allow to cool.
10.   Pipe or spoon a little whipped cream into each profiterole, then dip into the chocolate sauce.
11.   To serve, pile the profiteroles into a pyramid on a pretty plate and serve the rest of the chocolate sauce separately.

F The profiteroles can be frozen for up to 2 months. Thaw for 1 hour at room temperature.

Chocolate profiteroles; Viennese curd cake with apricot sauce

COFFEE WALNUT CREAMS

Makes 12

2 tablespoons golden syrup
1 egg white, stiffly beaten
25 g (1 oz) walnuts, finely
  chopped

FILLING:
25 g (1 oz) butter
50 g (2 oz) icing sugar
1 level teaspoon coffee essence

PREPARATION TIME: 15 minutes
COOKING TIME: 45-60 minutes
OVEN: 120°C, 250°F, Gas Mark 2

The unfilled biscuits will keep crisp for 2-3 days if kept in an airtight tin. They do not freeze.

1.   Place the golden syrup in a saucepan and bring gently to the boil.
2.   Remove from the heat and pour slowly on to the egg white, beating all the time. Fold in the walnuts.
3.   Using a teaspoon, heap walnut-sized mounds of the mixture on to a baking sheet lined with non-stick silicone paper.
4.   Bake in a preheated oven for 45-60 minutes until a dark brown colour. Leave to cool.
5.   To make the filling, beat the butter, icing sugar and coffee essence together and sandwich between the biscuits.
6.   Serve in sweet paper cases.

CHERRY TARTLETS WITH ALMOND PASTRY

Makes 24

225 g (8 oz) plain flour, sifted
pinch of salt
75 g (3 oz) icing sugar
75 g (3 oz) ground almonds
175 g (6 oz) butter, softened
1 egg, beaten

2 teaspoons cornflour
1 × 425 g (15 oz) can red
  cherries, drained and stoned
300 ml (½ pint) double or
  whipping cream, whipped

PREPARATION TIME: 40 minutes, plus chilling
COOKING TIME: 15-20 minutes
OVEN: 180°C, 355°F, Gas Mark 4

Many other soft fruits can be substituted for the cherries.

1. Place the flour, salt, icing sugar and ground almonds in a bowl and mix together thoroughly.
2. Rub in the butter until the mixture resembles fine bread-crumbs. Add the beaten egg a little at a time and knead well to form a smooth dough. Chill for 30 minutes.
3. Roll out the pastry on a floured surface. Cut out with a 5 cm (2 inch) fluted cutter and use to line patty tins.
4. Prick the pastry cases with a fork and bake blind in a preheated oven for 15-20 minutes until a pale golden colour. Cool on a wire tray. ⏹F
5. Mix the cornflour with a little of the cherry juice. Add to the rest of the juice and bring to the boil, stirring constantly. Simmer for 3 minutes until thick and syrupy.
6. Add the cherries and allow to cool. Fill the pastry cases with the cherry mixture.
7. Place the cream in a piping bag fitted with a 1.25 cm (½ inch) star nozzle and pipe a rosette on top of each tartlet. ⏹A

⏹F The pastry cases can be frozen for up to 2 months. Thaw for 30 minutes at room temperature.
⏹A The tartlets can be filled several hours in advance.

VARIATIONS:
If fresh cherries are in season, use these instead of canned cherries, stoning them first before use. Whipped double cream piped into the empty pastry shells and decorated with fresh fruit provides an exciting alternative finish to the above, and does not need a glaze. For a refreshing filling, peel, slice, core and cut fresh pineapple into segments, combine with a small quantity of whipped cream, and place in the pastry shells. Top each tartlet with a small segment of glacé cherry.

Top: Coffee walnut creams; *Bottom:* Cherry tartlets with almond pastry

From the top: Caramelized fruits; Mini meringues; Fruit kebabs

CARAMELIZED FRUITS

Makes 12-16

CARAMEL:
175 g (6 oz) granulated sugar
4 tablespoons water

FRUIT *(2 or 3 of each of the*
following):
satsuma segments

pineapple pieces, fresh or
tinned
cherries (optional)
strawberries
grapes, preferably seedless
lychees, fresh or tinned

PREPARATION TIME: 30 minutes

The caramelized fruits should be prepared and eaten on the same day. Choose fruits that are colourful. Where possible, leave on stalks to make dipping in syrup easier and to make the fruits easier to eat. Do not try to do too much fruit at once – you may have to make up a new batch of syrup.

1.   In a saucepan dissolve the sugar and water over a low heat.
2.   Boil rapidly until the syrup starts to turn a very light brown, then remove from the heat, otherwise it will burn.
3.   Spear each piece of fruit that does not have a stalk with a cocktail stick and carefully dip in the caramel. Place on non-stick silicone paper to set.
4.   Arrange the fruits in sweet cases, with or without cocktail sticks, and serve on a pretty plate. Keep in a dry place until required.

DESSERTS

MINI MERINGUES

Makes 30 shells

4 egg whites
225 g (8 oz) caster sugar

TO DECORATE:
300 ml (½ pint) double or

whipping cream, whipped
1 kiwi fruit, peeled, sliced and
cut into triangles (optional)

PREPARATION TIME: 15-20 minutes
COOKING TIME: 40-45 minutes
OVEN: 140°C, 275°F, Gas Mark 1

1.   Whisk the egg whites until very stiff, then whisk in half of the sugar. Gently fold in the remaining sugar.
2.   Put the meringue into a piping bag fitted with a 1 cm (½ inch) star nozzle. Pipe small circles of the meringue on to baking sheets lined with non-stick silicone paper or lightly greased greaseproof paper.
3.   Bake in a preheated oven for 40-50 minutes. Cool on a wire tray. F
4.   Sandwich the meringues together with a little whipped cream.
5.   Decorate each meringue with a small triangle of kiwi fruit, if using, and pile on to a serving dish.

F The meringues can be frozen unfilled for up to 3 months. Thaw at room temperature for 1 hour.

FRUIT KEBABS

Serves 20

1 fresh pineapple, peeled and
   cut into cubes
3 oranges, segmented and
   halved
100 g (4 oz) seedless green
   grapes
100 g (4 oz) black grapes,
   halved and pipped

100 g (4 oz) fresh cherries,
   stoned
2 firm kiwi fruit, skinned and
   cut into cubes
100 g (4 oz) strawberries

TO DECORATE:
sprigs of fresh mint leaves

PREPARATION TIME: 25 minutes

1.   Thread the prepared fruits on to cocktail sticks, paying special attention to colour combination.
2.   Arrange on a plate and serve as soon as possible.

INDEX

Almond and pineapple
    cheeses 85
Anchovy puffs 26
Apple slices 17
Artichoke dip 80
Asparagus and blue cheese
    filling 55
Asparagus rolls 49
Avocado pear 17
    Avocado and prawn
      sandwiches 47
    Avocado dip 81

Bacon 9
    Devils on horseback 78
    Egg and bacon rolls 84
    Mushroom, bacon and
      cheese quiches 27
Barbecue dip 72, 73
Bean salads 17
Beef, contrefilet of 73
Beignets, mushroom 58-9
Bread 13, 18
    see Rolls; Sandwiches
Bread sticks with Parma
    ham 55
Bread tartlet cases with
    fillings 55
Brisling envelopes 36
Butter, serving 13

Caper dip 63
Caramelized fruits 92
Carrots 16, 19
Caviar and cream cheese
    canapés 30
Celeriac 17
Celery boats, stuffed 59
Cheese 12-13, 14
    Almond and pineapple
      cheeses 85
    Asparagus and blue
      cheese filling 55
    Baby quiches 27
    Caviar and cream cheese
      canapés 30
    Cheese and ale toasties 54
    Cheese and ham fingers
      29
    Cheese balls with olives
      60-1
    Cheese shells 84
    Cheese whirls 24

    Cream cheese and
      pineapple topping 45
    Mushroom, bacon and
      cheese quiches 27
    Potted cheese 82-3
    Spinach and cheese
      quiches 27
    Spinach cheese puffs 35
    Stuffed dates 83
    Tomatoes stuffed with
      cream cheese and
      chives 60
Cherry tartlets with almond
    pastry 91
Chicken:
    Chicken and ham vol-au-
      vents 28
    Chicken and vegetable
      terrine 41
    Chicken drumsticks 71
    Curried chicken choux
      puffs 24-5
    Curried chicken eccles 32
    Hawaiian chicken 69
    Herby chicken with
      cucumber dip 80-1
Chicken livers:
    Ham cornets with liver
      pâté filling 74
    Hot liver pâté 37
Chocolate 19
    Chocolate cases with
      ginger syllabub 87
    Chocolate profiteroles
      88-9
    Chocolate sauce 88, 89
Choux pastry 24-5
Cocktail sausages with
    mustard dip 77
Cocktail Scotch eggs 79
Coffee walnut creams 90
Cornish pasties, miniature
    78
Country terrine of
    vegetables 40-1
Courgette salad 17
Courgettes stuffed with
    taramasalata 64
Crab and smoked salmon
    rolls 66
Croûtes, fried 53
Crudités, potted cheese
    with 82-3
Cucumber 16, 19
    Cucumber and yogurt
      salad 67
    Cucumber boats with
      prawns 57

Cucumber dips 58, 80-1
Curried chicken choux puffs 24-5
Curried chicken eccles 32
Curry and mushroom vol-au-vents 28

Dates, stuffed 83
Devils on horseback 78
Dips 9
    Artichoke 80
    Avocado 81
    Barbecue 72, 73
    Caper 63
    Cucumber 58, 80-1
Dolmas 61
Drinks 20-1
Duck:
    Terrine de canard aux raisins 38

Eggs:
    Cocktail Scotch eggs 79
    Egg and bacon rolls 84
    Egg and cress sandwiches 46
    Egg and prawn vol-au-vents 28
    Scrambled egg and chives on fried croûtes 52
    Stuffed eggs with prawns 65

Farmhouse pâté 39
Finger rolls 45
Flower arrangements 11
Freezing food 8-9
Fruit kebabs 93
Fruits, caramelized 92

Garnishes 18, 19
Gherkin fans 19
Ginger syllabub 87
Glacé cherries 19
Glasses 21
Goujons of sole 64

Ham:
    Bread sticks with Parma ham 55
Cheese and ham fingers 29
Chicken and ham vol-au-vents 28

Ham cornets with liver pâté filling 74
    Ham roulades 48
    Melon balls with Parma ham 73
    York ham with peaches 68
Hawaiian chicken 69
Hazelnut torte 86
Herb garnishes 18
Herby chicken with cucumber dip 80-1
Hot dogs, oven 56

Kebabs, fruit 93
Kebabs, mini 77

Lemon butterflies 19

Mackerel pâté 42
Meat balls, savoury 72-3
Melon balls with Parma ham 73
Meringues, mini 93
Mousse, tuna fish 43
Mushrooms:
    Curry and mushroom vol-au-vents 28
    Fresh mushroom mélange 83
    Mushroom, bacon and cheese quiches 27
    Mushroom beignets with cucumber dip 58-9
    Samosas 34-5
    Stuffed raw mushrooms 58

Parties: useful suggestions 6-15
Pasties, miniature 78
Pâté (see also Terrines):
    Farmhouse pâté 39
    Hot liver pâté 37
    Liver pâté and tomato sandwiches 47
    Mackerel pâté 42
Peanut sablés 31
Pineapple:
    Almond and pineapple cheese 85
    Caramelized pineapple 92
    Cream cheese and pineapple topping 45

Pinwheels 18, 48
Piping 18, 19
Pizzas, mini 50-1
Potted cheese 82-3
Prawns:
  Cucumber boats with
    prawns 57
  Egg and prawn vol-au-
    vents 28
  Stuffed eggs with prawns
    65
Profiteroles, chocolate 88-9

Quiches, baby 27

Radish roses 19
Radish waterlillies 19
Rollmops on pumpernickel
  62
Rolls 13
  Asparagus 49
  Egg and bacon 84
  Finger rolls with toppings
    45
  Smoked salmon and crab
    66

Salads 16-17
Salami cornets 76
Salmon:
  Salmon and cucumber
    sandwiches 47
  Smoked salmon and crab
    rolls 66
  Smoked salmon triangles
    44
Samosas 34-5
Sandwiches 9, 46-7
Sausages 9
  Cocktail sausages with
    mustard dip 77
  Oven hot dogs 56
Scampi, deep fried, with
  caper dip 63
Scotch eggs, cocktail 79
Scrambled egg and chives
  on fried croûtes 52
Sending invitations 6
Shortcrust pastry 27
Skordalia 50
Sole, goujons of 64
Spinach and cheese quiches
  27
Spinach cheese puffs 35
Syllabub, ginger 87

Table arrangements 10-12
Taramasalata:
  Courgettes stuffed with
    taramasalata 64
  Taramasalata on fried
    croûtes 49
Terrines (see also Pâté) 8
  Chicken and vegetable 41
  Terrine de canard aux
    raisins de Corinthe 38
Toasted bread and garlic 52
Toasties, cheese and ale 54
Tomatoes 16
  Tomatoes stuffed with
    cream cheese and
    chives 60
Tongue, pressed 74-5
Toppings, piping 18
Tuna and caper fillings 55
Tuna crescents 33
Tuna fish and mayonnaise
  topping 45
Tuna fish mousse 43
Turkey, roast, with lemon
  stuffing balls 70-1

Vegetables:
  garnishes 18, 19
  Chicken and vegetable
    terrine 41
  Country terrine 40-1
  Samosas 34-5
Viennese curd cake with
  apricot sauce 88
Vol-au-vents 28

York ham with peaches 68

ACKNOWLEDGEMENTS

Photographer: Ian O'Leary.
Stylist: Marian Price.
Food: Michelle Thomson.
Colour illustrations: Sue Lines.
Line illustrations: Paula Bayne.